HOPE FOR A DESPAIRING WORLD

HOPE FOR A DESPAIRING WORLD

The Christian Answer to the Problem of Evil

Philip E. Hughes

A CANTERBURY BOOK

Baker Book House
Grand Rapids, Michigan

For
HARVEY WHITE
F.R.C.S.

Copyright 1977 by
Baker Book House Company

ISBN: 0-8010-4159

Printed in the United States of America

CONTENTS

CHAPTER ONE
The Human Predicament

The early years of this twentieth century were years of un-bounded optimism — at least for those who had the good fortune to belong to the well-clad and well-fed classes of society in our western civilization. Given the confident assurance that man had risen from the humblest of biological (or nonbiological) origins and was perfectible to an infinite degree, the conviction reigned that nothing could stop his progress to ever more glorious heights. It is true that the First World War of 1914-18 gave a rude jolt to this op-timism, for the destruction of the flower of Europe's manhood starkly demonstrated that the fratricidal spirit of Cain was far from being a fault that had been left behind with the uncouth beginnings of man's supposed ascent to the status of a cultured and sophisticated being. But the conflict was conveniently rationalized as the "war to end war" and the League of Nations was founded with due solemnity as the guarantee that peace would now prevail for all time.

It could hardly be expected, however, that this attitude of optimism would be shared by the millions within our western civilization who eked out a drab existence below the poverty line in the overcrowded slums of the big cities and industrial areas, or by the still greater numbers of those beyond, in what is now called the "third world," whose existence was a constant losing struggle with disease and malnutrition. For many such, a spark of hope was ignited by the new voice of Communism, which attributed all the evils befalling the poor to their exploitation by the privileged few, promised the equal distribution of all wealth, and cheered them with the utopian vision of a classless — and godless — society from which the stupefying fumes of rank and religion had been dispelled.

Communism called to the "workers of the world" to unite, and to rise and seize their rights so that the new order of society might be established. The vision of Marx and Lenin was as materialistic and this-worldly as it was irreligious. While their philosophy approved an evolutionary (naturalistic) doctrine of the origin of man, their banner was essentially a revolutionary banner. What it might take evolution millennia to achieve, revolution would accomplish with dispatch. And indeed, in the two brief generations since Communism raised its head it has spread by persuasion and conquest, so that now it holds sway over the lives of hundreds of millions of the earth's population. Far from being a liberating force, however, it has imposed inhumanity and enslavement on the multitudes. Its absolutism is far more oppressive than anything known under the czars. "Equality" has turned out to mean no more than the suppression of individualism, the unreasoning conformity of the masses to the overbearing will of the party leaders, and the confiscation of property in the name of "collectivization." Nonconformity, or "deviation," is ruthlessly met with "correction" in the grim prisons and concentration camps and "mental" hospitals that form the Gulag Archipelago of Soviet Russia (not to mention other lands under Communist domination), of which Solzhenitsyn has written so revealingly, and from firsthand experience. There is evidence in plenty, and it is incontestable, that huge numbers of inoffensive human beings have been deprived of all freedom and are being cruelly tormented and done to death in the "utopias" of atheistic Communism.

Meanwhile in our "civilized" western world the futility of the League of Nations soon became apparent. It weakly watched the brutal rape of Ethiopia by Mussolini and of one country after another by Hitler, until, only two decades after its founding, World War II broke out — a conflict which proved to be considerably more global in extent than World War I. It not only cost, as before, the lives of millions of combatants, but also sanctioned the indiscriminate saturation bombing, by both sides, of densely populated cities with their noncombatant inhabitants, culminating in the devastation of the atomic holocaust at Hiroshima. The three decades since the end of World War II have witnessed savage and long drawn out warfare in Korea and Vietnam, fierce and repeated hostilities in the Near East, and internecine bloodshed on the Indian subcontinent and elsewhere. We have seen the development of the merciless tactics of terrorism, in all of which the helpless and the innocent have been the victims of brutality and destruction. The United Nations Organization, magnificently housed in its palace of boredom, is proving as ineffective as its predecessor. Paralyzed by grandiloquent vetoes and misused as a parade ground for petty nationalisms, the United Nations is virtually ignored by the world's potentates and diplomats.

There is nothing really exceptional in all this bloodshed and brutality, apart from the fact that the lethal weapons of our day are technically more sophisticated and devastating than those of past ages. "Civilization," as the soliloquist says in Dostoyevsky's *Notes from the Underground,* "has made mankind, if not more bloodthirsty, at least more vilely, more loathsomely bloodthirsty." The history of mankind all along has been marred by savage tyrannies and bestial inhumanities which have been inflicted in order to gain or retain power and to obliterate those who are regarded as enemies. Depraved and ambitious men have never been squeamish about the slaughter of the innocents. Domineering nations have always spent more on warfare than on welfare. Man seems to have an insatiable appetite for the destruction of his fellow men.

But international hostility is only part of the story. The common life of man is clouded and imperiled by crime and corruption of every kind. Selfish greed has driven our race to pollute the earth, the rivers, the seas, and the atmosphere which form our environment. Everything man touches he perverts. The astonishing scientific advances of this century have been used for the bane rather than the blessing of mankind. The promise of nuclear energy carries with it the threat of nuclear annihilation. The development of the oxygen lung is accompanied by the invention of napalm. The airplane which provides rapid transportation for millions is also a vehicle of death and mutilation for millions. Despite their great potential as media of news and culture, radio and television are abused as instruments of lying propaganda and misinformation. On all sides, fear, suffering, poverty, perversion, and exploitation are only too apparent. Even the conquest of outer space vastly expands the opportunities for international espionage and the raining down of destruction on the cities and peoples of our planet. Each new conquest of man extends the range of his propensity for evil.

WHY DOES GOD NOT DO SOMETHING?

Now the question is: How does, how can God fit into this picture? If indeed there is a God, why does he not declare himself and do something to put right so much that is wrong in his world? To a Christian alone and tormented in a dark Communist prison the satanic temptation comes: "I saw such deep sorrow in the world of this God that I said to myself, 'He has a heart of stone; otherwise he would ease the difficulties of the way for us.' . . . Innocent men are burnt alive in furnaces. And heaven is silent. It lets things be. Can God wonder if, in undertones, even the believers begin to doubt?"

Yet the believer who is suffering for Christ's sake cannot continue in doubt. He is never without the answer, for the answer is within himself, in that inward Power and Presence by which his life has been transformed and by which through every affliction he is sustained; so that temptations of this kind cannot prevail against him. Truly, as the same writer declares, under such duress "there are no lukewarm Christians; either you are a whole-hearted Christian or you are not a Christian at all, because it costs too much to be a disciple of Jesus." And so his true testimony is this: "In our darkest hours of tortures the Son of man came to us, making the prison walls shine like diamonds and filling the cells with light . . . . The spirit rejoiced in the Lord. We would not have given up this joy for that of kingly palaces."

Consider the following incident when, despite its inhuman foulness, a Communist prison was transmuted into a place of joy:

Aristar died in February. We had to dig through deep snow and break ground like iron to bury him in the prison yard, alongside Abbot Iscu, Gafencu, Bucur, and a score of others he had known in Room Four. His bed was taken over by Avram Radonovici, who had been a music critic in Bucharest.

Avram knew long passages from the scores of Bach, Beethoven, and Mozart, and could hum them for hours — it was as good as a symphony concert. But he had brought a more precious gift with him. Because of his tuberculosis, which had affected his spine, he was encased in a plaster cast when they brought him to Tirgul-Ocna, and as we watched he pushed a hand into the breast of this grey shell and extracted a small, tattered book. None of us had seen a book of any kind for years. Avram lay there quietly turning the pages, until he became conscious of the eager eyes fixed on him.

"Your book," I said. "What is it? Where did you get it?"

"It is the Gospel according to St. John," said Avram. "I managed to hide it in my cast when the police came for me." He smiled. "Would you like to borrow it?"

I took the little book in my hands as if it were a live bird. No life-saving drug could have been more precious to me . . . . The Gospel went from hand to hand. It was difficult to give it up . . . . Many learnt the whole Gospel by heart and we discussed it every day among ourselves . . . . This Gospel helped to bring many to Christ.[1]

The answer possessed by the believer is, however, unknown to the unbeliever. Yet the unbeliever is in no position to pass judgment on God, or to dismiss him as nonexistent, simply because he observes much that is wrong and unjust in the world. He presupposes, instinctively, that there is an absolute standard in accordance with which persons or conditions may be described as just or unjust, true or false, right or wrong. This standard is the ground of his complaint against God, and the implications of this presupposition are of considerable significance, as C. S. Lewis came to recognize.

1. Richard Wurmbrand, *Tortured for Christ,* pp. 44, 45; *In God's Underground*, pp. 103f.

"My argument against God was that the universe seemed so cruel and unjust," he says with reference to the atheistic period of his life.

> But how had I got this idea of *just* and *unjust*? A man doesn't call a line crooked unless he has some idea of a straight line. What was I comparing this universe with when I called it unjust? If the whole show was bad and senseless from A to Z, so to speak, why did I, who was supposed to be part of the show, find myself in such violent reaction against it? A man feels wet when he falls into water, because man isn't a water animal: a fish wouldn't feel wet. Of course I could have given up my idea of justice by saying it was nothing but a private idea of my own. But if I did that then my argument against God collapsed too — for the argument depended on saying that the world was really unjust, not that it just didn't happen to please my private fancies. Thus in the very act of trying to prove that God didn't exist — in other words, that the whole of reality was senseless — I found I was forced to assume that one part of reality — namely my idea of justice — was full of sense. Consequently atheism turns out to be too simple. If the whole universe has no meaning, we should never have found out that it has no meaning: just as if there were no light in the universe and therefore no creatures with eyes we should never know it was dark. *Dark* would be a word without meaning.[2]

But there still remains the fact of the existence of evil as well as good in the world. Granted that God exists, how are we to account for this unequal state of affairs? Christians, after all, profess to believe in God's sovereignty over the whole of creation. Unitedly, as they recite the creed, they affirm belief in "God the Father Almighty, Maker of heaven and earth and of all things visible and invisible." Things being as they are, is there any possible justification for such a belief? If God really is sovereign, why are things as they are? Is he, as the deists used to teach, an absent God who set the

---

2. C. S. Lewis, *Broadcast Talks,* pp. 40f.

whole universe in motion but now watches from afar, unconcerned as history runs its uneven course? It is impossible to suppose that, being God, he cannot take action. But, surely, that *he cares not* is just as unthinkable as that *he can not*. How could God possibly cease to care for his creation? Is it not evident that the disintegration of the world he has made must mean also the frustration of his purposes in creating it? It cannot be imagined that God intended his creation to fall away from himself into anarchy and godlessness and perdition. But where then is the evidence of his concern and of his power?

These are not new questions. Three thousand years ago the Psalmist felt his faith faltering as he compared the afflictions suffered by the righteous with the prosperity enjoyed by the wicked. It all seemed so unjust. "My feet had almost slipped," he wrote, "my foothold had all but given way, because the boasts of sinners roused my envy when I saw how they prosper." He could not help remarking that "their slanders reach up to heaven, while their tongues ply to and fro on earth," as they mockingly ask: "What does God know?" and scornfully reply: "The Most High neither knows nor cares"; and that, despite such arrogance, "yet still they prosper, and rogues amass great wealth," while at the same time God's faithful servants "suffer torment." Is all the Psalmist's piety and dedication then in vain? But he is aware that even to entertain such a thought is to "betray the family of God." "So," he says, "I set myself to think this out, but I found it too hard for me."

A PROBLEM TOO HARD FOR MAN

This was a problem the Psalmist could not solve as long

as he made himself and his fellow men the measure of things. As soon, however, as he prostrated himself before God in his sanctuary he saw things in their true perspective: the wicked are on slippery ground and judgment comes upon them suddenly and with dreadful finality. "I found it too hard for me," he testifies, "until I went into God's sacred courts; there I saw clearly what their end would be." He saw clearly, moreover, that God was ever with him to uphold and to bless him, that God himself was his true reward, and that having God he had everything, indeed that his glorious destiny was to be everlastingly in the presence of his God. And so he ended his psalm with these memorable words of confession and commitment:

> When my heart was embittered
> I felt the pangs of envy,
> I would not understand, so brutish was I,
> I was a mere beast in thy sight, O God.
> Yet I am always with thee,
> thou holdest my right hand;
> thou dost guide me by thy counsel
> and afterwards wilt receive me with glory.
> Whom have I in heaven but thee?
> And having thee, I desire nothing else on earth.
> Though heart and body fail,
> yet God is my possession for ever.
> They who are far from thee are lost;
> thou dost destroy all who wantonly forsake thee.
> But my chief good is to be near thee, O God;
> I have chosen thee, Lord God, to be my refuge. (Psalm 73) [3]

Similarly, in Psalm 37 the God-fearing man is admonished not to be disturbed at the prosperity of wicked persons, nor to emulate their methods and standards of success.

---

3. With the exception of occasional variations the translation used throughout is that of the New English Bible.

"It is the Lord who directs a man's steps," the Psalmist reminds us; "he holds him firm and watches over his path." Adversity may indeed meet the godly man in his way; but, "though he may fall, he will not go headlong, for the Lord grasps him by the hand." Consequently, true wisdom consists in following this counsel: "Turn from evil and do good, and live at peace for ever; for the Lord is a lover of justice and will not forsake his loyal servants." It is unfailingly true that "deliverance for the righteous comes from the Lord, their refuge in time of trouble" (Ps. 37:23f., 27f., 39).

Why is it, then, that at times of deepest need, when the darkness of despair seems impenetrable, God gives the impression of being inattentive to the prayers of his people? Surely at such times some sign of his concern, some display of omnipotence, would reasonably be expected. Why does God not open the heavens for us as he once did for Stephen, and encourage us with a vision of the victorious Jesus at the right hand of the majesty on high (Acts 7:55f.)? Why does he withhold any token that he cares? This was certainly the situation in which the apostles imagined that they found themselves when their small boat on the lake was in imminent danger of being swamped by the waves that were breaking over it. Jesus was in the stern *asleep* (!) and apparently quite unconcerned about the catastrophe which stared them in the face. "Master, we are sinking!" they cried. *"Do you not care?"* Guilty of a failure both of nerve and of faith, they stood rebuked as with a word he calmed the raging elements. We can well understand that "they were awestruck and said to one another, 'Who can this be? Even the wind and the sea obey him!' " (Mark 4:36ff.). Thus they were taught that what appeared to them an insuperable problem was no problem at all for him through whom the world and all its elemental forces were brought into being.[4]

Still more anguished and despairing, if possible, was the perplexed complaint of Martha and, in turn, Mary when Jesus arrived in Bethany after the death of their brother Lazarus: "O, if you had only been here my brother would not have died" (John 11:21, 32). This complaint, it is true, shows confidence in Jesus as the healer of the sick. But in their hour of need, despite the fact that they had sent a special message to inform him that his friend Lazarus was seriously ill, he had delayed coming to them until it was too late. He of all people had failed them in this hour of crisis. And so Lazarus had succumbed to the illness and his corpse had been laid in the tomb. Jesus had come too late; for we all stand helpless before the inexorable finality of the cold clutch of death.

Yet, appearances notwithstanding, Jesus was not only compassionately concerned but also at every moment completely in control of the situation. This the disciples had learned when by his word of power he had reduced the tempest to stillness. Now he so ordered things that his followers would understand that he was lord over death as well as lord of the elements. His delay in coming was deliberate, and its purpose was "for the glory of God." That is why he was able, even after receiving the news of Lazarus' death, to say to his disciples: "Lazarus is dead. I am glad not to have been there; it will be for your good and for the good of your faith" (John 11:4, 14f.). Belatedly, then, as Martha and Mary saw it, but actually at the precise moment of the divine timing,[5] he came to Bethany and by his coming the scene of

---

4. See John 1:3, 10; I Corinthians 8:6; Colossians 1:16; Hebrews 1:2f.

5. Cf. Galatians 4:4.

blank human despair was transformed as he made the place
of death the opportunity for the manifestation of God's
loving power. The authority of his word was such that even
the dead man heard and responded and was restored to life.
The lesson is plain: that faith must never waver, not even in
the face of death. Hence the challenge of Jesus to Martha: "I
am the resurrection and the life. If a man has faith in me,
even though he die, he shall come to life; and no one who is
alive and has faith shall ever die. Do you believe this?" (John
11:25f.).

We are back once again at the perspective of the
Christian believer, the principle of whose existence is faith in
God and confidence in his word. And it is to this perspective
that we shall constantly return, since it is the only perspective
with inner coherence and consistency. The perspective of the
believer is radically different from that of the unbeliever. It
is true, as we have seen, that even the God-fearing man is
tempted to question God because of the injustices of human
society or because of the dark days of affliction through
which he himself may be passing; but, as we have also seen,
this temptation cannot destroy the reality of his experience of
divine grace. To question the goodness of God is, in essence,
to imply that man is more concerned about goodness than is
God. The man who knows God cannot do this, for he knows
that the God whose grace he has received is the source of all
goodness. To suggest that man is kinder than God is to sub-
vert not only the godly man's profession and inward experience (whatever his outward circumstances may be) but
also the very nature of God (which of course is unaffected by
human falsehood). It is to deny God; and this is precisely the
thrust of the temptation to question the goodness of God.
The satanic desire is to turn the godly man back into an
ungodly man. Again and again we must heed the age-old in-

terrogation: "Can mortal man be more righteous than God, or the creature purer than his Maker?" (Job 4:17). For man to demand that God should justify himself to his creatures is a devilish overturning of the right order of things.

LET GOD BE GOD

As P. T. Forsyth has said, "The first, last, and supreme question of the soul, of religion when it is practical, is not, 'How am I to think of God?' . . . but it is, 'What does He think of me?'" And he continues:

> More positively it is, 'How shall I be just with God? How shall I stand before my judge?' That is the final human question — how to face the eternal moral power. What is it making of us? What is He doing with us? What is He going to do? That is the issue in all issues. That question of Judgment is where all other questions end. It is the central question in religion, How shall I stand before my judge? So much is this the case, so inevitable, capital, and final is this function of judgment, that if God be not owned as man's judge, man becomes God's. Where man is not felt to be on his trial before God, God is put on His trial before man, and summoned to explain Himself to the conscience of the time.[6]

It is man who must give an account of his ways to God, not God to man — though, as in due course we shall further explain, God has certainly not left man without ample witness to his goodness and power. Accordingly, the Lord asked his afflicted servant Job:

> Is it for a man who disputes with the Almighty to be stubborn?
> Should he that argues with God answer back?

To this Job responded:

> What reply can I give thee, I who carry no weight? I put my finger to my lips . . . .

---

6. P. T. Forsyth, *The Cruciality of the Cross,* p. 59.

Again, out of the tempest the Lord put this question:

> Dare you deny that I am just or put me in the wrong that you may
> be right?

And finally Job made this confession:

> I know that thou canst do all things and that no purpose is beyond
> thee. But I have spoken of great things which I have not un-
> derstood, things too wonderful for me to know . . . . Therefore I
> despise myself; I repent in dust and ashes. (Job 40:1-8; 42:1-6)

In other words, as Luther insisted, we must let God be God.

The ungodly man, however, is in rebellion against God. He accepts the satanic invitation to question God's goodness and ignore his word, and welcomes the assurance that in so doing he himself will become like God. He believes that in setting out along the road of the knowledge of good and evil, he will have before him the glorious vista of independence and self-determination.[7]

Generation after generation man plays at being God. He sets himself up as the center of reality and the fount of wisdom to whom even God is accountable. Arraigned before the bar of man's judgment, the Almighty is found wanting and is admonished that the world is better able to get on without him. God, it may be, served some purpose during the ages of man's immaturity when there was perhaps need of the comfort afforded by myths of a power beyond himself. But now, we are assured on all sides, man has come of age. He is secular man living in a demythologized world; he is scientific man who contrives and controls the machinery of the future. Accordingly, it is no longer the life but the death of God that man celebrates.

But in point of fact, as Jacques Ellul has penetratingly argued, the old sanctities have but been replaced by new

---

7. See Genesis 3:1ff.

ones; for modern atheistic man is a fanatically religious being. He has invented new and contradictory myths which he holds absolutely sacred. In his worship of the new gods of scientism and libido, statism and revolution, he finds himself torn between the polarities of law and license, of conduct that is structured and conduct that is unstructured. It is not Christianity, indeed, which needs to be demythologized but the technological and libertarian faith of contemporary society. It is the Christian gospel alone which can effect the exorcism of the demons which have possessed the soul of modern man.[8]

Despite all his claims to sophistication and self-adequacy, modern secular man has not found it possible to do without the aid of miracles. For example, he has resorted to the mythical primeval miracles of spontaneous generation, by virtue of which, it is postulated (in defiance of every scientific principle, for this is a case of blind faith), life was first produced from lifeless matter. And he claims that the supreme achievement of the long miraculous process that followed so incredible a beginning is man himself — secular, scientific man. Thus he regards himself as the crown of the system and the lord of the future, the personal product of an impersonal force called Nature. The personal Creator whom he has dismissed from his creed is supplanted by the myth that it is Nature, not God, that plans and brings into being, and provides and makes perfect.

Other radical adjustments to the creed have also, of course, been necessary. Divine election, for example, whereby God orders all things in accordance with his perfect will and wisdom, has been replaced by natural selec-

---

8. Jacques Ellul, *Les Nouveaux Possédés*. See also Os Guinness, *The Dust of Death*.

tion, which with uncanny efficiency assumes responsibility for the upward progress of things. In this connection, as a matter of fact, there has been a considerable alteration even in the creed of naturalism. The earlier concept of a steady inevitability of progress has been discarded in favor of a doctrine of spasmodic advance by means of the selective appropriation of chance mutations which happen to be advantageous to the upward drive. It is conveniently overlooked that when mutations occur they are usually deleterious and even lethal in their effects, so that, to say the least, natural selection is an improbable doctrine.

This notion of progress by accident is tantamount to whistling in the dark to keep one's spirits up. It reflects the degree to which the erstwhile serenely confident optimism of the humanist has been shaken by the upheavals and disasters of the last sixty years and by the unstable and unpromising state of human society that now prevails. It gives expression to the desperate desire that somehow good may come out of evil. If the survival of the fittest (now a matter of chance) has been written into the creed in place of the final perseverance of the saints, affirmation of trust in the lottery of mutation has also been substituted for the assurance of the benign immutability of the purposes of God.

CHANCE OR CERTAINTY?

The setting up of chance in the place of certainty is eloquently symptomatic of the sickness of our age. It is hardly surprising that some have found it preferable to deny not only hope for the future but also a pattern for the past, and have proclaimed a world that is chaotic in its incoherence. The philosophy of nihilistic existentialism, for instance, asserts that the whole is without meaning and that man is adrift on a shoreless sea. This view holds that everything, past or present, which is separate from the individual's own existence has no reality for him. The only possibility of authenticity lies in the determined affirmation of his own existence and the passionate choice of that over which he has no choice, his future, and especially the inevitability of his own death and annihilation. This attitude of desperate defiance rises from the depths of the lostness and alienation which modern man experiences as he finds himself trapped in the meaningless vortex of his and society's futility. Having declared his own self-adequacy, he is unwilling to admit that the frustration of his powerlessness is the inescapable consequence of his denial of the power and thus, in effect if not in word, the existence of God. He refuses to see the chaos both of his own life and of human society as a self-induced judgment on his and its godlessness.

To conclude that this situation is peculiar to our age would be a mistake. It is characteristic of human fallenness in all ages and in all places. But in our day the intensity of the human predicament is increasing in a shrill crescendo. Blasphemies are poured forth in sound and in print. Indecencies that once were shameful and private are now publicly displayed and praised. Perversions are condoned and indeed encouraged as part of the rich variety of personal fulfillment available to man. The abnormal is treated as normal. Materialism, lust, and violence are becoming the hallmarks of our civilization, which seems increasingly intent on rushing headlong down the Gadarene slope into the abyss of total anarchy and permissiveness.

Strident voices seek to persuade us that good is evil because it restricts our freedom of choice and action, and that evil is good because it expands the horizon of our experience. The original sin in the garden, we are advised, is symbolical of human progress since the fruit of the tree of the knowledge of good and evil is more desirable than the fruit of the tree of life, and the eating of the former placed in man's hands the determination of his own destiny, a prize for which expulsion from the garden was a small penalty to pay. Besides, the knowledge of evil, it is said, is necessary for progress. It is beneficial in the long run. We learn by our mistakes. Did not Nietzsche teach us a hundred years ago that God is dead and that "man is a rope, fastened between animal and Superman — a rope over an abyss," that "this is the great noontide . . . when man stands at the middle of his course between animal and Superman and celebrates his journey to the evening as his highest hope, for it is the journey to a new morning"?[9] We move onward and upward, the fashioners of human destiny. In this we are assisted, as we have already noted, by the sleepless activity of that numinous power known as natural selection in the elimination from the system of all that is harmful and deleterious. And so we are invited to fix our gaze on the distant vision (of little comfort to us who are swallowed up in the mid-course of the process) of a future that is free from fault — which, ironically, brings man back to the garden where everything is very good and from which it was essential that he should escape in the first place! Thus the whole procedure has the appearance of a colossal exercise in futility!

Meanwhile, however, it cannot be denied that crime is increasing at an alarming rate, that society is haunted by insecurity, and that the utopian vision is becoming not less

---

9. Friedrich Nietzsche, *Thus Spake Zarathustra*.

but more distant. Even so, many allow themselves to be persuaded that the present convulsions are only for the time
being, that they are the birth pangs of a better and juster
state of affairs, that they are to be understood as a harsh
but necessary means of casting aside an establishment which
is effete and unacceptable. We are asked to believe that the
quest for social justice sanctifies lawlessness. "We all know
what it is," says Razoumikhin in *Crime and Punishment,*
with reference to the socialists and their theory of crime;
"crime is a protest against a badly organized social state of
things — that's all . . . . In their opinion, man is driven to
commit crime in consequence of some irresistible cen-
trifugal influence. This is their favorite theme."[10]

Certainly this is no new theme. Yet it is self-evident that
crime contributes to rather than corrects the degeneration of
society. None the less, this continues to be today, as it has
been in the past, the theme of the revolutionary as he attempts to justify the use of unjust means in the campaign
against the injustices of society. The seeds of defeat are
present even in victory, so that the bitter crop which is cut
down springs up again. There stalks through human history
a tragic nemesis which man has set in motion and from
which he is powerless to escape. His pursuit of blessedness
is clouded by the presence of a curse.

Today it has become customary to regard the criminal
as sick rather than guilty. Violence and corruption are sen-
timentalized as things dictated by a man's genes and re-
inforced by his environment. The blame is laid, too, on the
provocation of the moment. In serious cases it is now a
familiar line of defense that the accused person was not

---

10. Fyodor Dostoyevsky, *Crime and Punishment.*

responsible for his actions, or was in a state of "diminished responsibility" at the time of the offense. It follows that if a man is not responsible for what he has done he cannot be declared guilty and be punished, since guilt and punishment necessarily imply responsibility.

HUMAN RESPONSIBILITY

There is, of course, no question that upbringing and environment as well as reaction to the stress of a particular situation may be important considerations in the assessment of a man's conduct and character. But to deny his responsibility is hardly a kindness to the criminal or a service to society. It is, rather, to dehumanize the offender, for responsibility is of the very essence of humanness. It is, moreover, as anarchical as it is dehumanizing, since law and order and common decency are meaningless concepts apart from the reality of the responsibility of human society and its members. Guilt or innocence is established on the basis of responsibility. Justice is accomplished by the clearing of the innocent and by the punishment of the guilty. Injustice would be accomplished by clearing the guilty and punishing the innocent.

Yet on all sides we hear the concept of criminal guilt and its desert of just punishment or retribution denounced as vengeful and inhumane. The offender, it is urged, is sick rather than wicked, and a man cannot be blamed and punished for being sick. Sickness is not penalized: it is treated. According, then, to this "humanitarian" theory (as C. S. Lewis called it) verdicts of guilty and punitive sentences should not be pronounced on offenders; being sick and the victims of forces beyond their control, they must be sent off for "treatment." The true victim of crime is overlooked. There is already ample evidence of the way in which this therapeutic benevolence may be tyrannically extended beyond corrupt and violent persons to those who are politically or ideologically or religiously out of line in the eyes of officialdom, and who consequently are placed behind prison walls or in the wards of "mental" hospitals ostensibly for the purpose of being "treated" and "cured."

Those who deny the reality of God and his justice are precisely the ones who deplore the notions of guilt and punishment in human relations. The very awareness, as we have observed, of rightness and wrongness, of guilt and innocence, implies the existence of an absolute standard of justice which, since these concepts relate to the realm of personal interaction, must belong to One who is himself supremely personal. It should not surprise us that atheistic materialism with its "humanitarian" dismissal of guilt and punishment is dehumanizing and depersonalizing in its outworking, and that its methods of correction are deliberately destructive of the minds and wills of men until in the end they cease to be truly human persons. Furthermore, the attempt to eliminate the concepts of guilt and punishment from the human scene is symptomatic of the wish of the ungodly man to escape from the reality of his own guilt and from the judgment he himself deserves as one who has broken the laws of God, before whom he and all others must stand and give an account. In his rebellion against the sovereignty of God he desperately desires to persuade himself that there is no such thing as eternal retribution hereafter. And so he denies at the temporal level what he fears at the eternal level.

But to shut one's eyes at midday and then to assert that, because one perceives only darkness, the sun is not shining or even is nonexistent does not for one moment alter the fact that the sun is indeed there, pouring forth light and heat from on high. Unbelief is closing one's eyes to the truth: it is self-induced blindness, the refusal to see and acknowledge the truth that is there all the time concerning the sovereign Creator who is the sole source of the life and light of our being. Such unbelief is wicked because it is wilful; it is culpable because it is rebellious. It involves the suppression of the truth — not just some truth of secondary importance, but that truth which is of absolute significance because it is fundamental to the right understanding of ourselves and our place in the universe, namely, the truth *about God*. The apostle Paul, in fact, insists that the presence of violence and corruption in human society is itself a sign of God's judgment in action here and now and a warning of final judgment hereafter. He writes, "We see divine retribution revealed from heaven and falling upon all the godless wickedness of men" (Rom. 1:18). And their wickedness consists essentially in this: that they are "stifling the truth," since "all that may be known of God by men lies plain before their eyes." This truth about God is not hidden or withheld from them, for none other than "God himself has disclosed it to them." The evidence surrounds them on every side; for the logical precision of the working of the universe, of which man himself is a part, testifies daily and inescapably both to the mind of the Maker and also to his eternal power and deity as the sovereign Lord of all creation. "His invisible attributes," says St. Paul, "that is to say his everlasting power and deity, have been visible ever since the world began, to the eye of reason, in the things he has made" (Rom. 1:19f.).

The cosmic harmony of the whole is everywhere apparent. It is something from which man cannot isolate himself. It silently but none the less emphatically witnesses to the mind of man about the Mind of the Creator. Everywhere it is eloquent concerning the sovereign glory of God. "The heavens tell out the glory of God," sings the Psalmist, "the vault of heaven reveals his handiwork. One day speaks to another, night with night shares its knowledge, and this without speech or language or sound of any voice. Their music goes out through all the earth, their words reach to the end of the world" (Ps. 19:1-4). The suppression of this ubiquitous truth is inexcusable. "There is therefore no possible defence," says Paul, because, "knowing God, they have refused to honour him as God, or to render him thanks" (Rom. 1:20f.). This mutinous ingratitude in the face of the goodness and grace of the Creator is the complete antithesis of the attitude of the godly man, or in other words the regenerate man, who desires his whole life, here and hereafter, to be the expression of his gratitude to his divine Redeemer and heavenly Father.

SUPPRESSING THE TRUTH

Of course, to suppress the truth about God is at the same time to suppress the truth about myself; for my essential existence as creature implies my total dependence on God as Creator and demands my grateful acknowledgment of him as the source and sustainer of my existence, if I am to have a right understanding of myself: who I am, how I am, and the meaning of my existence. To rebel against God, to be self-centered, is to sever the lifeline that links me to him and to drift away into meaninglessness. To assert independence where dependence is native not merely to my true being but also to the true expression of my humanity is nothing less than suicidal. It is the greatest possible folly, the choice of unreason instead of reason, of darkness instead of light, of death instead of life. "Hence all their thinking has ended in futility, and their misguided minds are plunged in darkness," declares Paul of those who have turned their backs on God. "They boast of their wisdom, but they have made fools of themselves, exchanging the splendour of immortal God for an image shaped like mortal man, even for images like birds, beasts, and creeping things" (Rom. 1:21-23).

The apostle is speaking, of course, of the practice of *idolatry*. As God's creature made in the image of God, man is by constitution a *religious* creature (of this more will be said in the next chapter), and his revolt against God does not alter what he is by nature. His nature is to worship, and if he does not worship the one true God he must needs invent a false god for the satisfaction of his religiousness. Consequently, since all that is not God belongs to the realm of creation, the idolater worships an inferior creature instead of the supreme Creator. Moreover, as no created thing of any kind can begin to be a substitute for the infinite Creator, what he worships is a no-god. The incredible folly of idolatry is graphically described by the Psalmist:

> Why do the nations ask,
> "Where then is their God?"
> Our God is in high heaven;
> he does whatever pleases him.
> Their idols are silver and gold,
> made by the hands of men.
> They have mouths that cannot speak,
> and eyes that cannot see;
> they have ears that cannot hear,
> nostrils, and cannot smell;
> with their hands they cannot feel,
> with their feet they cannot walk,

and no sound comes from their throats.
Their makers grow to be like them,
and so do all who trust in them. (Ps. 115:2-8)

Similarly, the message of the prophet Isaiah to the people of
his day was unmistakably plain:

Thus says the Lord, the creator of the heavens,
he who is God,
who made the earth and fashioned it . . . .
I am the Lord, there is no other . . . .
You fools, who carry your wooden idols in procession
and pray to a god that cannot save you! . . .
There is no god but me;
there is no god other than I,
victorious and able to save.
Look to me and be saved,
you peoples from all corners of the earth;
for I am God, there is no other. (Isa. 45:18-22)

Today we pride ourselves because we no longer bow
down to graven images. Idolatry, however, is by no means a
thing of the past; it is just that we have grown accustomed to
more sophisticated, though still ancient, forms of idolatry:
the worship of money, devotion to pleasure and the lusts of
the flesh, the veneration of material possessions and luxury,
the cult of worldly success and prestige, adoration of the
state or of a political party. But these are just as much no-
gods as are graven images. Man's religion, his god, is that
for which he lives, and if his is not the worship of the true
God it is the worship of the creature. And the worship of
created things can never satisfy the deep religious need of the
human heart; indeed, it is destructive of authentic human
dignity, leading as it inevitably does, since man was made for
communion with the true God, to the degradation of society
and to existence without ultimate meaning.

Moreover, departure from God brings its own retribution. Those who harden their hearts against the truth and

of set purpose give up God have no ground for complaint if God in turn gives them up. To be given up by God is a terrible consequence of turning away from God. The reality of this abandonment displays itself in social anarchy and the perversion of human relationships. This, in fact, is the key to understanding the evils with which human civilization is beset. Three times in the passage from which we have already quoted Paul affirms that God has *given up* those who defiantly have turned their backs on him. "For this reason," Paul says,

> God has given them up to the vileness of their own desires, and the consequent degradation of their bodies, because they have bartered away the true God for a false one, and have offered reverence and worship to created things instead of to the Creator, who is blessed for ever.

And again:

> In consequence, I say, God has given them up to shameful passions. Their women have exchanged natural intercourse for unnatural, and their men in turn, giving up natural relations with women, burn with lust for one another; males behave indecently with males, and are paid in their own persons the fitting wage of such perversion.

And yet again:

> Thus, because they have not seen fit to acknowledge God, he has given them up to their own depraved reason. (Rom. 1:24-28)

This apostolic diagnosis of the human situation is so plain that none can mistake its meaning. It should give pause to those who today, within the church as well as elsewhere, condone and even encourage the practice of homosexuality, as though it were an acceptable norm for those who are so disposed and not rather the catastrophic disintegration of human sexuality. Homosexual relationships, it is true, are but one symptom of the chaotic disruption that prevails in the community of mankind when the divine will is neither honored nor acknowledged. The parading of nudity and lewdness on and off the stage is another symptom of man's ungodly mockery of the shame of his fallenness. The mark of Cain has become all too familiar to us as society, both national and international, is tormented by hatred, violence, and fratricide; for ungodly man is also unbrotherly man: he becomes insanely fratricidal. In short, the depravity of those who refuse to honor God, and whom God has given up, "leads them to break all rules of conduct." And the catalog of viciousness which Paul adds could hardly sound more contemporary to us:

> They are filled with every kind of injustice, mischief, rapacity, and malice; they are one mass of envy, murder, rivalry, treachery, and malevolence; whisperers and scandal-mongers, hateful to God, insolent, arrogant, and boastful; they invent new kinds of mischief, they show no loyalty to parents, no conscience, no fidelity to their plighted word; they are without natural affection and without pity. They know well enough the just decree of God, that those who behave like this deserve to die, and yet they do it; not only so, they actually applaud such practices. (Rom. 1:28-32)

GIVEN UP BY GOD

But, it may be objected, it would seem that by *giving up* ungodly persons to the outworking of their own viciousness and hostility God is following the line of least resistance and withdrawing himself from responsibility for the evil which mars the world he has made. To allow things to go from bad to worse, so far from affording a solution to the problem, appears to be self-defeating and even to argue incompetence on the part of God. This, however, is a misreading of the situation. Paul does not present the whole picture in this passage, but only one aspect of it. The later chapters of Romans will explain how God does indeed act decisively for the restoration of his creation and the final judgment of all godlessness in accordance with his will and purpose. In any case, the "giving up" of which Paul speaks does not imply a failure of action on God's part, but rather a deliberate procedure whereby the judgment that flows from God against his rebellious creatures is seen to be in operation even now, prior to the enactment of final judgment. That is why Paul says that "we see divine retribution revealed from heaven" — here and now (present tense) — "and falling upon all the godless wickedness of men" (v. 18). Their rebelliousness fails completely to establish their independence of God; on the contrary, it places them under the cloud of his displeasure which will at last burst in a storm of destruction, but from which even now showers of judgment are already falling. The conclusion of the passage shows, furthermore, that ungodly men are aware of the inevitability of the ultimate judgment which will overtake them: "They know well enough the just decree of God that those who behave like this deserve to die, and yet they do it" (v. 32).

Present as well as ultimate retribution is the nemesis which overtakes evildoers. It is, so to speak, a built-in factor from which, apart from the response of repentance and faith to the grace of God, there is no escape. The man who sells his soul to the idol of lust, whether it be the lust of the flesh or the lust for money or the lust after worldly position and power, always discovers that his idol is incapable of fulfilling what it promises. Lust always ends by sating and sickening its devotees. Bitter disillusionment is the wage it pays; for the ungodly man learns at last the hollowness both of his excesses and also of his successes, which leave him "a pauper in the sight of God" (Luke 12:21). This nauseating retribution came upon the rebellious Israelites in the wilderness when they lusted after meat.

You wailed in the Lord's hearing [Moses told them]; you said, "Will no one give us meat? In Egypt we lived well." The Lord will give you meat and you shall eat it. Not for one day only, nor for two days, nor five, nor ten, nor twenty, but for a whole month you shall eat it until it comes out at your nostrils and makes you sick; because you have rejected the Lord who dwells in your midst, wailing in his presence and saying, "Why did we ever come out of Egypt?" (Num. 11:18-20)

Thus, always, lust turns to disgust.

The same principle is discernible in the history of nations and civilizations which, after attaining power and prosperity, become self-corrupted by a taste for idle luxury and for the entertainment provided by spectacles of violence and sensuality. Augustine observes, for example, that the great civilization of Rome, whose downfall he witnessed in his day, "had more reason to regret the departure of its poverty than of its opulence, because in its poverty the integrity of its virtue was secured, but through its opulence dire corruption, more terrible than any invader, took possession not of the walls of the city but of the mind of the citizenry."[11] And in his most famous work, the writing of which he undertook on receiving the news that the Goths had sacked the "eternal city" of Rome (A. D. 410), he reminds the Romans that their own statesman Scipio "did not consider a republic to be flourishing whose morals were in ruins, though its walls were standing."

But [he continues] the seductions of evil-minded devils had more influence with you than the precautions of prudent men . . . . Depraved by good fortune and not chastened by adversity, what you desire in the restoration of peace and security is not the tranquillity of the commonwealth but the impunity of your own vicious luxury. Scipio even wished you to be hard pressed by an enemy so that you

---

11. Augustine, *Letter 138*, to Marcellinus.

might not abandon yourselves to luxurious manners; but you are so abandoned that your luxury is not repressed even when you are crushed by the enemy. You have missed the profit of your calamity; you have been made most wretched, and yet have remained most profligate.[12]

Warning voices have very properly drawn attention to the striking similarities between the condition of society at the time of Rome's collapse and the moral and materialistic corruption that is now so obviously eating at the heart of our western civilization. Arthur Koestler, indeed, perceives that we have already gone beyond this analogy: "The basic novelty of our age," he writes, "is the combination of (the) sudden, unique increase in physical power with an equally unprecedented spiritual ebb-tide."[13]

It may very well be said that on all sides we see the increase of vice and violence and the perversion of justice, and it is undeniable that great suffering is brought on mankind by human arrogance and selfishness, indeed that the corrupt state of society is a divine judgment invited by our ungodly ways. The remarkable penetration of the biblical diagnosis of the sickness with which our world is afflicted must be acknowledged. But why does God allow this undesirable state of affairs to persist? The New Testament predicts, in fact, that things are going to get worse, not better.

The final age of this world will be a time of troubles. Men will love nothing but money and self; they will be arrogant, boastful, and abusive; with no respect for parents, no gratitude, no piety, no natural affection; they will be implacable in their hatreds, scandal-mongers, intemperate and fierce, strangers to all goodness, traitors, adventurers, swollen with self-importance. They will be men who put pleasure in the place of God, men who preserve the outward

12. Augustine, *City of God,* I.33.

13. Arthur Koestler, *The Sleepwalkers,* p. 540.

form of religion, but are a standing denial of its reality. (II Tim. 3:1-5)

If indeed things are going from bad to worse this only strengthens the force of the objection, for it seems to indicate that God's grip on the situation is slackening, that the reins are slipping from his hands. If he is really sovereign, ought he not to cause things to get better instead of worse? Why (the question is asked again) does he not intervene to put things right and to establish harmony and justice in his world? Why does he not take decisive action to eliminate evil once and for all from his creation?

THE LONG-SUFFERING OF GOD

We may not have a ready answer to all such questions. God certainly has his reasons for allowing things to be as they are, and his reasons, though hidden from us, are always good reasons. Moreover, Christ's admonition to the apostles still holds good for us in our day: "It is not for you to know about dates or times, which the Father has set within his own control" (Acts 1:7). This much may be asserted, however, that God's delay (as it seems to us) is our opportunity to return to him, for it is prompted by his long-suffering: "It is not that the Lord is slow," Peter writes, ". . . but that he is very patient with you, because it is not his will for any to be lost, but for all to come to repentance" (II Peter 3:9). Instead, therefore, of complaining about God's apparent failure to take action, we should be grateful to him for his forbearance and should not ourselves delay to come to terms with his gracious offer of new life in Christ Jesus. Otherwise the wisdom to which we pretend proves to be the greatest stupidity (Rom. 1:21f. again!), since by our censure of God's supposed incompetence we exclude ourselves from the very thing we most need, namely, his grace and his blessing which, thanks to his long-suffering patience, continue to be available to us. To heed the appeal of the prophet would be true wisdom:

> Inquire of the Lord while he is present,
> call upon him while he is close at hand.
> Let the wicked abandon their ways
> and evil men their thoughts:
> let them return to the Lord, who will have pity on them,
> return to our God, for he will freely forgive.
> For my thoughts are not your thoughts,
> and your ways are not my ways.
> This is the very word of the Lord.
> For as the heavens are higher than the earth,
> so are my ways higher than your ways
> and my thoughts than your thoughts. (Isa. 55:6-9)

Thus the history of God's "delay" coincides with the era of his grace, for it is the history of the period in which the message of the gospel is proclaimed throughout the world's length and breadth (cf. Acts 1:8) and in which God calls out a people for himself, of whom it is said: "You are now the people of God, who once were not his people; outside his mercy once, you now have received his mercy" (I Peter 2:9f.). The rough fisherman is transformed into Christ's ambassador, the money-loving tax collector into an evangelist, the self-righteous Pharisee into the apostle to the Gentiles. Augustine, whose indulgence in sensual passion had left him disgusted, who had tested and found wanting the claims of philosophy and astrology, and who on coming to Milan could not escape the challenge of Ambrose's preaching, sent an anguished cry to heaven: "How long, how long must it be tomorrow, always tomorrow? Why not now? Why not this very hour an end to my baseness?" Then, taking up a manuscript of Paul's letters, he read: "No revelling or drunkenness, no debauchery or vice, no quarrels or jealousies! Let Christ Jesus himself be the armour that you wear; give no more thought to satisfying the bodily appetites.''[14] This, for Augustine, was the moment of passing from defeat to victory; the end of his search for the truth, for reality, for the meaning of everything; the beginning for him of new life in Christ, in whom he found the key to the understanding of his own existence and of his place in the eternal purposes of God. And so throughout human history God's grace and power combine in the transformation of lives. It is thus that God salts the world to preserve it from total corruption and causes his light to shine and hold back the darkness of man's depravity. The sway of God over the life of an individual is a token and a gauge of his sway over the whole of creation.

God, then, is indeed intervening in the affairs of this world through those whose lives are touched by his goodness and through the instrumentality of his church. In this way human wickedness is held, as it were, at the end of a rope. But this continuous intervention in personal and social life itself rests upon and flows from the fact that he has already intervened in a decisive and sovereign manner in the past, and points to the certainty that he will intervene no less decisively, and this time finally, in the future. These crucial interventions, both past and future, are effected through Jesus Christ, who at his first coming appeared in his capacity as Redeemer and at his second coming will appear in his capacity as Judge. And we must not lose sight of the further fact that God originally "intervened" by taking action in the creation of the world, and that this too was effected by the

---

14. Augustine, *Confessions,* Book 12; Rom. 13:13f.

agency of the Son, through whom all things came into being. The rest of this book will be devoted to a consideration of the sovereignty of God and the infallible power of his action under these three main headings: Creation, Redemption, and Judgment.

First, however, it must be emphasized that God's action, whether in creation, redemption, or judgment, precisely because it is *God's* action, cannot fail to be effective. In other words, it is important for us to know just what we mean when we speak of God. The powerlessness of the churches today is in large measure attributable to the fact that preachers and theologians have in one way or another reduced the size of God. They have presented a God who is too small.[15] Some, indeed, have reduced him to merely human proportions. But the infinity of God cannot be diminished. God, by definition, is the Supreme, the Infinite, the Eternal Being who as such necessarily exercises absolute sovereignty over the whole of his creation. This is the meaning of the term *God*, and if we speak of God in lesser terms we in fact cease to speak of God at all and are speaking instead of a figment of man's imagination or a projection of his arrogance. If, therefore, we speak of God, we are speaking of him who is supreme over all. To challenge the sovereignty of God is to challenge God himself. To confine God within any degree of relativity or contingency is (theoretically) to dethrone him and to bring all things under the chaotic uncertainty of uncontrolled chance. Hence the confusion that man brings into his life and into society at large when he mutinously sets himself up as the master of things. Under God, however, all things are without exception

---

15. See J. B. Phillips, *Your God Is Too Small.*

fully controlled — despite all appearances to the contrary. For God not to be completely sovereign would be a contradiction in terms. Accordingly, when God in his sovereignty takes action, as he has already done and as he will yet do, he cannot fail to do so in a manner that is altogether effective for the fulfillment of his will and purpose.

CHAPTER TWO
The Creation of Man

The first need of man is summed up in the ancient admonition, "Remember your Creator" (Eccles. 12:1) — that
is to say, "Acknowledge your creatureliness and give God
the honor that belongs to him alone." To understand the
beginning is to understand the end, for the end is in the
beginning; and to lose the beginning is to lose the end also
and the whole meaning of things by which the end is bound
to the beginning.

The key to the mystery of existence is present in the
opening words of Holy Scripture: *"In the beginning God."*
We must start with God or we do not start at all in our comprehension of reality. To leave God out of the picture is to
lose the picture. God is eternally there, before the beginning
and at the beginning, and also as the One who is responsible
for the beginning of the world. Accordingly, the primary
statement continues: "In the beginning *God created*" — by
his sovereign power he brought into being that which
previously had no being — *"the heavens and the earth,"* the
totality, in other words, of this universe of which man is a
part (Gen. 1:1; cf. Eph. 3:9). The knowledge of this truth
should cause God's creatures to praise him without ceasing,
as in the celestial vision given to John: "Thou art worthy, O

Lord our God, to receive glory and honour and power, because thou didst create all things; by thy will they were created, and have their being'' (Rev. 4:11).

As the maker is master of what he has made, so God is sovereign over the whole of his creation. To the eye of the prophet the work of creation in all its diversity is like the potter's molding of clay into vessels of different design according to his will: "Lord, thou art our father; we are the clay, thou the potter, and all of us are thy handiwork'' (Isa. 64:8). For the creature to criticize his Creator is no less absurd than the thought of an earthen vessel criticizing its maker. Thus God speaks through Isaiah as follows:

Will the pot contend with the potter,
or the earthenware with the hand
that shapes it?
Will the clay ask the potter what he is making?
or his handiwork say to him, "You have no skill''?
Will the babe say to his father, "What are you begetting?'',
or to his mother, "What are you bringing to birth?''
Thus says the Lord, Israel's Holy One, his maker:
Would you dare question me concerning my children,
or instruct me in my handiwork?
I alone, I made the earth and created man upon it;
I, with my own hands, stretched out the heavens
and caused all their host to shine. (Isa. 45:9-12)

Created reality is the expression of the divine will, and skill, and in its cosmic harmony it reflects the ordered perfection of the divine mind. This evidence of God's power and wisdom, as we have seen (Rom. 1:19f.), is visible to all. It should call forth not our criticism but our worship; we should join with the Psalmist in singing:

Bless the Lord, my soul:
O Lord my God, thou art great indeed,
clothed in majesty and splendour . . . .
Countless are the things thou hast made, O Lord.

Thou hast made them all by thy wisdom,
and the earth is full of thy creatures. (Ps. 104:1, 24)

As, moreover, nothing that God does is aimless or futile or without purpose, so creation, designed in accordance with the will of God, is conformed to the purpose of its Creator. The world is not the consequence of caprice, a pretty toy to be played with and then discarded. God's purposes are sure, and his sovereignty is displayed precisely in the indefectibility of all that he purposes. A failure of his purpose would be a failure of his sovereignty. All things are *from* him and *through* him and *to* him, who is the "Source, Guide, and Goal of all that is" (Rom. 11:36). It is *for* him as well as *by* him that all things exist (Heb. 2:10). The divine purpose is the impulse of the whole of creation.

Just as it is unthinkable that God's purpose in creation should meet with frustration (for then it could not be *God's* purpose), so also it is unimaginable that God should abandon his creation or allow it to collapse into perdition. This again would mean the abandonment or the defeat of his purpose, which in turn would mean that he does not possess that sovereign supremacy that belongs to God alone, and therefore he could not be God after all. It would, as Athanasius wrote in the fourth century, be "inappropriate in the extreme" for God's work to come to nothing. But there is another development to be taken into consideration, namely, the entry of sin into God's world. When sin entered, creation was threatened with disaster. What, Athanasius asks, was God in his goodness to do when his rational creatures were perishing and his noble works faced with ruin?

> Was he to permit corruption to prevail against them and death to hold them in its grip? If so, what was the use of their being made in the beginning? It would have been better, rather, for them not to have been created than, once created, to be neglected and to perish.

For neglect and indifference to the ruination of his own work would argue weakness rather than goodness on God's part, much more so than if he had never made man at all. If he had not created anything, there would have been none to impute weakness to him; but once he had made things and brought them into being it would have been altogether preposterous for his work to perish, and that too before the eyes of their Creator. Therefore it was out of the question for God to leave men to be carried away by corruption: to do so would have been inappropriate and unworthy of his goodness.[1]

The manner in which God effects the restoration of his creation and achieves the fulfilment of all his purposes will be discussed in the two following chapters. Our concern, at this point, is to stress the utter foolishness of imagining that God could set aside his purposes by abandoning his creation and allowing it to pass unchecked into a state of corruption.

The work of God as Creator involves not only the act of bringing the world into being but also the continuous activity of keeping it in being. God *sustains* what he has made. A father who begets a son cares and provides for him; how much more does God care and provide for his creation! The universe, which was brought into being from nonexistence, would relapse into nonexistence if God should withdraw his care even for a moment. God the Son, however, who is the eternal Word through whom all things were made (John 1:3), also upholds the universe by his word of power and carries it onward to its destined goal.[2] This is what we mean when we speak of divine *providence*.

---

1. Athanasius, *The Incarnation of the Word of God,* § 6.

2. Cf. Hebrews 1:3: "the Son . . . sustains the universe by his word of power." The Greek verb translated "sustains" is not static but dynamic: he "bears it onward."

THE PROVIDENCE OF GOD

Providence is the corollary of creation; for the whole created order is totally dependent on God, not merely at the moment when it is brought into existence, but at every moment for the continuation of its existence. This truth is expressed poetically by the Psalmist when he speaks of God's creatures in the following words: "All of them look expectantly to thee to give them their food at the proper time; what thou givest them they gather up; when thou openest thy hand they eat their fill" (Ps. 104:27f.). Or again in another psalm:

Thou dost visit the earth and give it abundance,
as often as thou dost enrich it with the waters of heaven,
brimming in their channels, providing rain for men.
For this is thy provision for it,
watering its furrows,
levelling its ridges,
softening it with showers and blessing its growth.
Thou dost crown the year with thy good gifts
and the palm-trees drip with sweet juice;
the pastures in the wild are rich with blessing
and the hills wreathed in happiness,
the meadows are clothed with sheep
and the valleys mantled in corn,
so that they shout, they break into song. (Ps. 65:9-13)

The providence of God is seen, then, year after year, in the unfailing sequence of the seasons, in the blessings of sunshine and rain and the productivity of the earth, in seedtime and harvest. It is apparent also in the settled courses of the heavenly spheres in our solar system. Indeed, it is seen in the majestic orderliness of all things, whether it be the immensities of cosmic space with its physical constants, the distinctive patterns of the microscopic structures of the tissues of animal and plant life, or the marvelous designs even of inanimate matter. Still more wonderful, if possible, is the discovery that the basis or heart of all matter (so deceptively stolid and static in appearance) is *energy*, that every infinitesimal atom of matter is vibrant with the force of its own solar system, the potential energy of which is so vast as to be beyond our comprehension.

Such is the *dynamism* of God's creation! Everywhere, in things both great and small, we are confronted with the expression of the rationality of God. This alone explains the fact that, as Sir Edmund Whittaker has asserted, "reality is an interrelated system, possessing a rational and coherent structure"; and this in turn makes possible and justifies the factor of predictability in the realm of scientific research. To quote Whittaker further:

Predictability is a consequence of the existence of laws of nature. For instance, the places of the sun and moon and planets in the sky can be predicted by making mathematical calculations based on the law of gravitation. Moreover, the laws of nature themselves constitute the mathematical structure by which the physical universe is held together; in which statement we count among the laws of nature not only such regularities as the law of gravitation and the electromagnetic formulae, but also theoretical geometry. Thus the notion of reality involves the notion of predictability, the notion of predictability involves the notion of the laws of nature, and the laws of nature form a rational structure underlying nature; and we are finally led to conclude that reality is at every point in intimate relation with the structure, and that a knowledge of the structure may be used to determine fresh constituents of reality. It has, in fact, often happened that a discovery in physics has originated not in laboratory experiments but in mathematical reasoning; as was the case for instance with Hamilton's prediction of the conical refrac-

tion of light in biaxial crystals, or Einstein's prediction of the bend-
ing of light-rays in the sun's gravitational field.[3]

This "fundamental principle of the rational interconnectedness of reality"[4] simply testifies to the truth that
the rationality of creation is a reflection or manifestation of
the rationality of the Creator. All things, of whatever
magnitude, bear witness to the wisdom, the purpose, and
the power of Almighty God, who by his word has brought
them into being and who by the same word also providentially sustains his creation and bears it forward to the
destiny he has willed for it. The energy at the heart of every
particle of matter of which the universe is compounded is
eloquent testimony of that primary and absolute Energy of
the word of God's will which activates the whole order of
creation.

Yet it is plain, as we have observed in the preceding chapter, that there is a great deal that is wrong with the world, a
great deal that is unjust and disruptive. This is true in particular of the *human* situation; to understand how this has
come about it is essential that we should understand what has
happened to man. In the Genesis account of creation, man is
the last of God's creatures to appear and is the crown or
culmination of the created order. He has various similarities
to other creatures, but at the same time he is radically different from them. This radical difference is indicated in the
affirmation that man alone of all the creatures was made in
the image of God (Gen. 1:26f.).

---

3. Sir Edmund Whittaker, *The Modern Approach to Descartes' Problem*
(The Herbert Spencer Lecture in the University of Oxford, 1948), pp. 25,
26.

4. Ibid., p. 26.

MAN CREATED IN THE IMAGE OF GOD

The creation of man in the divine image is what sets him apart from and makes him superior to the rest of God's creatures. Man's constitution in the image of God, moreover, displays itself in a variety of ways; for, in a manner unique to himself in the physical world, man is a personal, rational, moral, regal, creative, and religious being. We shall discuss briefly each of these aspects of man's being; but first of all it must be emphatically stated that the doctrine of man's creation in the image of God does not imply an identity or community of being (an *analogia entis*) between man and God, as though man were a part or projection of the essence of God: God in his infinity, eternity, and absolute independence is totally other than man. What the doctrine does imply is that man as created by God enjoys special affinities and potencies which make possible, and indeed necessary for the full expression of his humanity, a privileged relationship and intimate fellowship with his Creator. The imprint of God's image upon man means that at the very heart of man's being, and constitutional to it, is the knowledge of this relationship and an awareness of the truth about God from which man can no more escape than he can escape from himself. It means that the true glory of man is to reflect in his life the glory of God. This distinctive character of his humanness sets him apart not only *from* God's other creatures but also *to* and *for* the loving and thankful service of his Creator.

First, then, the image of God in which man was created may be discerned in the fact that man is a *personal* being. He is capable, accordingly, of entering into a personal relationship with God, on a person-to-Person basis, since God also and supremely is a personal Being, whose personality is known to us by the distinction of the three Persons, Father, Son, and Holy Spirit, within the unity of the Godhead. This interpersonal relationship within the unity of the divine being means that God is essentially, though mysteriously, a personal Being, and self-sufficiently so. Man, by contrast, is a personal being in his relationship with others than himself — with his fellow human beings, certainly, but no less fundamentally in relationship with his personal Creator. The fulfilment of his personality requires, therefore, the vertical relationship with God as well as the horizontal relationship with his fellow man, the transcendental as well as the temporal. And the vertical comes first, because the horizontal follows from it. Hence the order of the two great commandments: to love God with all one's being and to love one's fellow man as oneself. For love is the true expression of personality, which discovers itself only in relation to another. *God is Love* (I John 4:9); he is Love because of the supreme and essential personality of his Being. The personality of man is the imprint of the divine Personality. By it he is enabled to transcend all the rest of creation and his own physical limitations. In man's temporal existence personality is the window of eternity. As Nicolas Berdyaev commented:

> The entire world is nothing in comparison with human personality, with the unique person of a man. Personality is a microcosm, a complete universe. It is personality alone that can bring together a universal content and be a potential universe in an individual form. That universal content is not to be attained by any other reality in the world of nature or of history.[5]

This uniqueness of man as a personal being declares also the

---

5. Nicolas Berdyaev, *Slavery and Freedom,* pp. 20, 21.

uniqueness of his potential, and therefore responsibility, for living as one who loves God and his neighbor.

Second, the fact that man is a *rational* being is further evidence of his having been created in the image of God. Because of his faculty of reason man is able to appreciate the orderliness of the universe to which he belongs and to recognize it as expressive of the rationality of God. Man's rationality relates him to God, not only as person to Person but also as mind to Mind, and particularly to God as the source of all reason, and therefore, also, of all wisdom and knowledge. The rationality of God, with which his whole creation is invested, makes possible the rationality of man. It is the mind of God that gives meaning to things. If the world were absurd and irrational, man, as part of this world, would himself be absurd and irrational. But it is thanks to the grand logic of the whole created order that man is able to conduct himself rationally as thinking man and scientific man; for, made in the divine image, he knows, instinctively and by his very constitution, that there is an interconnectedness of all things, that one fact leads on to another, that reality is coherent, that the world is not a fragmented chaos but a *cosmos* and a *universe* — in short, man is able, as it has been said, to think God's thoughts after him. Man's rationality, moreover, makes possible word-communication between God and himself, and between himself and his fellows. More particularly still, it means that there is a direct affinity between God's rational creature, man, and the divine Son, who, as the Word or Logos, reveals to man the mind and will of the Father, and effects that will.

Third, the image of God with which man is stamped displays itself in man's knowledge of himself as a *moral* creature. He is by nature conscious of the difference between right and wrong, justice and injustice, kindness and cruelty.

In other words, he is a being with a *conscience* which either sanctions or condemns his motives and his deeds (cf. Rom. 2:14f.). This moral sense is an inner voice demanding that man should conduct himself *responsibly* both as an individual in private and also in public as a member of the community of mankind. It provides a foundation for the administration of justice in courts of law (cf. Rom. 13:1ff.); indeed, it causes man to recognize that in every aspect of his daily life, in his professional and business associations, in his political and social relationships, and even in the games which he plays or watches, there are rules and regulations and standards to be observed, the infraction of which rightly incurs penalties of one kind or another. But, more than that, the fact that every person knows *within himself* that he is responsible for his conduct is an indicator that man is answerable to his Creator, the source of all morality and the supreme Judge of all, who implanted this moral sensibility within him and before whose judgment seat all must stand (Rom. 14:10). Man as a moral creature is intended to reflect on earth the absolute morality, righteousness, and holiness of his Creator. Hence the divine requirement: "You shall be holy, for I am holy" (Lev. 11:44f.; I Peter 1:16).

Fourth, the divine image is apparent in this, that man in relation to the rest of the created order is a *regal* being. He is endowed with a kingly function and capacity. His regal character is manifested in his ability to tame and train other creatures for purposes useful to himself, to harness the elemental forces and energies of nature, to promote the civilization of society, to adapt, to cultivate, to explore, to invent, and, in short, to look on the world as there to be mastered by him, as he in turn is mastered by God. Such remarkable potencies mirror the sovereignty of Almighty God and afford man the equipment, constitutional to his being, whereby he applies himself to the fulfilment of the divinely given mandate to subdue the earth and to rule over all other earthly creatures (Gen. 1:28). Thus the Psalmist praises God for crowning finite man with glory and honor, giving him dominion within the sphere of creation, and putting everything under his feet (Ps. 8:5f.). Because this faculty, far from being man's own achievement, has been entrusted to him by God, the dominion of man in God's world is to be exercised to the glory of God and in submission to his supreme will.

Fifth, the fact that man is a *creative* being testifies to the reality of the image of God in which he was made. God alone, of course, is creative in the sense that everything within the universe owes its existence to him. God alone brings things into being which before had no being. Man's creativity resides in his God-given ability to work creatively with the forces and materials that are ready at hand in the world, and comes to expression in the realms of art and music, literature and architecture, and in his capacity for mechanical inventiveness. Such creativity opens the door to the joyful appreciation of the beauty and wonder of God's universe and to the production of glorious new combinations of forms and sounds from the elements that are given within it. Thus man is privileged to identify himself exultantly with the harmony of the whole and to make his own expressive contribution to "all that is true, all that is noble, all that is just and pure, all that is lovable and gracious, whatever is excellent and admirable" (Phil. 4:8). Man's creative achievement, moreover, reaches the true height of satisfaction and fulfilment when, with all things else, it is pursued to the glory of him who is the sole source of all creativity.

Sixth, man is a *religious* being, and in this most of all the image of God in which he is constituted manifests itself.

Religiousness, which is not a mark of any other creature, is man's consciousness of his close relationship to God, his total dependence on God, and his answerability to God. It is the expression of man's constitutional need for communion with his Creator and of the logic which demands that his whole life should be a manifestation of his gratitude to God. The impulse to worship is fundamental to the nature of man. As we have already seen, even if man ceases to worship the one true God he does not cease to be a religious being: he still must worship; but he then becomes an idolater, worshiping false gods of one kind or another, and encompassing his life with futility. The great need of fallen man is to discover (or rediscover), as Augustine discovered, that God has formed us for himself and our heart is restless until it rests in him.[6]

THE TRAGEDY OF MAN

The tragedy of man is not that he was left in the darkness of ignorance to grope his way toward the truth, but quite the opposite, that, though by nature possessing the knowledge of the truth about himself and his Creator, he preferred darkness to light (John 3:19). At first, as the Genesis account of creation teaches, man was blessed with constancy of fellowship with his Creator and rejoiced in the harmony of the universe. But then the temptation came to doubt and to disobey the word of God, and, indeed, to think evil of God from whom he had received nothing but unalloyed goodness. The tempter subtly suggested that God was even threatened by man's presence in the garden, and that in consequence he

---

6. Augustine, *Confessions,* I.1.

had placed a prohibition on eating the fruit of one of the trees in order that, like an insecure tyrant, he might restrict man's freedom and hold him in subservience. The tempter persuaded man, further, that the warning that he would certainly die if he should eat the fruit of that tree was an empty warning, since, the tempter implied, God was powerless to enforce such a threat and in any case had no competence to predict what would or would not happen, because the future, being at the mercy of chance and contingency, was completely unpredictable.

And so the truthfulness of God, the source of all truth, was flatly denied — "Of course you will not die. God knows that as soon as you eat it, your eyes will be opened and you will be like God knowing both good and evil" (Gen. 3:4f.) — and man was invited to assert himself in defiance of God, to seize freedom for himself by demonstrating his independence of God, to increase the range of his knowledge by embracing evil as well as good, and to be his own god and master. But God remains God. The denial of his existence does not reduce him to nonexistence, nor does man's flaunting of authority render God powerless. The consequence of man's rebellion is not power and liberty but shame and confusion, alienation from his Creator, disharmony within himself and with his environment, and the loss of the meaning and purpose of his existence. The evil that was to liberate him haunts him wherever he turns and pollutes even the good that he wishes to do. Through his own folly he has brought a curse upon his existence, he has experienced disintegration at the very core of his being, and, having wilfully turned his back on Life, he now has Death staring him in the face. Far from being master of the world, or even of himself, he finds himself in bondage to the tempter who so falsely promised him a godlike existence (cf. Heb. 2:14f.). By believing the word of

Satan instead of the word of God he has allowed that creature who is the enemy of all good to usurp the place of the Creator. This is the primary idolatry, the worship of the creature instead of the Creator, which lies behind all other forms and expressions of idolatry, so much so that the devil is called by Jesus "the prince of this world" (John 12:31; 14:30; 16:11) and by Paul "the god of this passing age" by whom the minds of men have been blinded with unbelief (II Cor. 4:4).

THE PERVERSION OF THE DIVINE IMAGE

When man rebelliously defies the true God in whose image he has been created, refusing to honor him as God and to be thankful to him, it is only to be expected that the divine image which is constitutive of his being should be horribly abused and disfigured. Understanding this, we begin to understand the reason for the abundance of wickedness and violence in our world. The wish of the ungodly and self-centered man is to obliterate the divine image in which he is made, but he is powerless to remove what is constitutive of his being as man. He finds many ways, however, of corrupting and perverting the image, though in doing so he can hope for not the least success in shaking off the truth about God and his sovereignty. All that he achieves through his ungodliness is the degradation of his own humanity. It is he, not God, who suffers loss. Instead of dethroning God he is dehumanizing himself.

The ungodly man shows his depravity by the distorted use to which he puts every single aspect of the divine image in which he is made. As he frantically attempts to reverse the true order of things he persuades himself that God is made in the image of man, rather than man in the image of God. He wishes to fit all reality into a humanistic framework. *Personality* is manipulated, accordingly, so that it becomes the cult of *human* personality, whether the glorification of the dictator to whom hymns are religiously sung and grandiose statues erected, or the adulation of the "popular idol" before whom thousands pay their swooning homage. Yet the cult of personality can thrive only at the cost of the repression of the personal dignity of others. Man's tyranny over man, whether it be the tyranny of the megalomaniacal despot or of the faceless bureaucratic machine or of the monopoly of "big business" or of the officialdom of trade-unionism, always has a depersonalizing effect, depriving those who make up the multitude of their worth as individuals and with impersonal unconcern treating them as nonpersons. Thus, for example, the right to strike, which originally was designed for the benefit of all, has become an instrument in the hands of the few for forcing the many to cease work irrespective of their personal wishes, and thus for depriving them of the still more basic privilege of the right to work. The crude inhumanity of man's propensity for depersonalizing his fellow men is most starkly apparent in the calculated brutalities of totalitarianism and the police state and the callous atrocities of total warfare; but every act of self-aggrandizement by means of the uncaring exploitation of others contributes to the dehumanization of society. The reminder is more necessary than ever today that it is only in relationship to God, who is the supremely personal Being and who, as the source of all personality, is no respecter or exploiter of persons, but deals impartially with all at a Person-to-person level[7] (Job 34:19: "who does not show special

---

7. Cf. Acts 10:34; Romans 2:11; Galatians 2:6; Ephesians 6:9; I Peter 1:17.

favour to those in office and thinks no more of rich than of poor''), that human personality, both individual and collective, finds its true proportion and dignity.

The arrogance of the ungodly man who boasts of his *rationality* as though it were his own achievement, setting himself up as the fount of all reason and the originator of all wisdom, is also inexcusable. To behave in this way is, in effect, to deny the rationality and even the existence of the Creator; and nothing could be more irrational than to ignore him to whom we owe our rationality and every other faculty. The irrationality of the opponent of supernaturalism is evident in the dogmatism which asserts that the world is a closed system, functioning in accordance with its own built-in and self-developed natural laws, and not open to intervention "from without" or "from above," and which yet at the same time holds that this supposedly closed system is completely open to the future, since the future, being (it is postulated) at the mercy of blind chance and haphazard coincidence, is entirely unknown and unknowable — this amounts to holding that nothing unusual happens but that anything unusual can happen! Highly irrational, too, is the suppression of the truth concerning God, with whose rationality the whole universe is stamped, for, as we have already observed (Rom. 1:18ff.), the evidence of this truth stares man in the face on all sides and the knowledge of it is present within every man by virtue of the divine image in which he has been created. As Paul says, it is precisely *to the eye of reason* that the truth of the Creator's eternal power and deity is constantly visible. To deny this truth is regarded by the ungodly as a mark of superior wisdom, but, as the apostle affirms, the fact is that, despite their pretensions, those who do so ''have made fools of themselves''; in their humanistic pride they have preferred irrationality to the acknowledgment of the sovereign rationality of God, and have blinded themselves to the logic of the Logos which is the pure source of the light of every intellect (John 1:9).

The disfigurement of the divine image in its *moral* aspect is particularly obvious in these days when, to the accompaniment of the raucous clamor for total freedom of sexual expression, every conceivable type of immorality is praised and portrayed in books, on the stage, and in films (with or without the pretext that it is presented as honest art or serious literature); pornographic displays attract a numerous patronage; promiscuities and perversions of all kinds are claimed as normal for and by those who wish to practice them; indecent and blasphemous language is on the lips of many and in the ears of most; and addiction to devitalizing drugs is destroying the lives of great numbers of young people. The wave of wantonness which is sweeping through society is undoubtedly satanic in origin and dehumanizing in its effects, but, as we noticed in the preceding chapter, it should also be seen as a judgment which our civilization is bringing on itself by its departure from the moral standards prescribed for the welfare of mankind by the Creator who himself is absolutely holy. The denial of morality is at the same time an attempt to deny the answerability of man to his holy Creator. This is a terrible defilement of the divine image. There is an urgent need for godly persons not only to cultivate holiness, "without which no one will see the Lord" (Heb. 12:14), but also to call on society to honor and to return to the observance of those laws and standards which God has given for the regulation of human conduct. This, however, is not solely a matter of human relations, though personal and public morality is essential to the health of society; it is a matter also of honoring God, who in the perfection of his holiness demands the response of holiness from us his creatures. Certainly, for those who profess to serve God and to love their fellow men the issue is plain, for, as Paul says, the whole moral law is summed up in love (Rom. 13:10). Further, "God called us to holiness, not to impurity. Anyone therefore who flouts these rules is flouting, not man, but God" (I Thess. 4:7f.). And Peter writes:

> As obedient children, do not let your characters be shaped any longer by the desires you cherished in your days of ignorance. The One who called you is holy; like him, be holy in all your behaviour, because Scripture says, "You shall be holy, for I am holy." (I Peter 1:14ff.)

EXPLOITATION AND ANARCHY

In his ungodliness, moreover, it is not only himself that man pollutes but also the earth over which God has given him *regal* dominion. The mandate to subdue it and to rule over its creatures (Gen. 1:28) intended that man should govern the world, under God, justly and wisely, establishing harmony and prosperity in every place, so that the concord between the Creator and his creatures might be reflected in the concord between man and man and between man and the rest of the natural realm. But the revolt against God, whereby man imagines he can assert his kingly supremacy and independence to an absolute degree, has inevitably led to the misuse of that regal faculty which belongs to the divine image in which he was fashioned. Instead of exercising this faculty to the glory of God, and in dependence on his sovereign will, man has become obsessed with egomania and the lust for power, with the result that the history of human rule has repeatedly been a history of tyranny and corruption and selfish enrichment at the expense of those over whom ascendancy has been gained. And man ruthlessly exploits the rich resources of the earth no less than he does his own kind. With undiscriminating greed he digs up and cuts down the vegetation and destroys the animal life of land and water; he covers over the good earth with the concrete artificiality of the human megalopolis; he fills the atmosphere with the deadly fumes from his machines and poisons the rivers and the seas with the waste products of his factories; and he intensifies the complex economic problems of society by the proliferation of vast and expensive bureaucracies which, ironically, are set up for the purpose of curing and controlling those very problems. Such is the shape of man's dominion over this earth. It is a sad defacing of the divine image. In refusing to acknowledge God as his King ungodly man has subverted his own kingly function and has involved the world over which he has been placed in the anarchy of his own lostness.

The fallenness of man is confirmed, further, by the degree to which the wonderful potential of his *creative* faculty is given over to the invention of ever more fearsome instruments of conquest and destruction. While the brilliance of such "achievements" may not be denied, the deep contradiction at the heart of mankind is eloquently attested by this yoking together of creativeness and destructiveness. It would be difficult to imagine anything more incongruous. Again, the lending of one's creativity to the production of "art" that is distorted and ugly, of "music" that is discordant and unmeasured, and of "literature" that is coarse and debasing — so much a phenomenon of our day — may well be an expression of the anguish and disharmony at the heart of modern man who has lost his way in a world made alien and hostile by ungodliness; but it also testifies to the depravity to which man can descend, to the failure of dignity and nobility which results when he turns away from God, the fountainhead of all beauty and harmony, and to the willingness with which he prostitutes the creative gift afforded by the divine image.

Departure from the worship of him who is "the King of all worlds, immortal, invisible, the only God" (I Tim. 1:17), is the cause also of the *religious* chaos of our world. Man, the religious creature, fashioned for fellowship with his Creator, cannot cease to be what he is constitutionally by reason of the image after which he has been formed. As has already been said, when he abandons the worship of the true God he will turn to the worship of false gods, who are no-gods, and who therefore can never satisfy the religious needs at the heart of his being. Jeremiah rebuked the people of his day for following "gods powerless to help" — "they were no gods." The prophet denounced the prevailing apostasy in the following terms:

My people have exchanged their glory
for a god altogether powerless.
Stand aghast at this, you heavens,
tremble in utter despair, says the Lord.
Two sins my people have committed:
They have forsaken me, the source of living water,
and they have hewn out for themselves cisterns,
cracked cisterns that can hold no water. (Jer. 2:8-13)

A people that persists in religious infidelity plunges itself into the dark depths of superstition and devotes itself to observances and beliefs which are as degrading as they are futile and powerless. A God-forsaking society becomes a God-forsaken society. Hence the stern words of Jeremiah to his compatriots in explanation of the disaster which was then coming upon them:

Your forefathers forsook me, says the Lord, and followed other gods, serving them and bowing down to them. They forsook me and did not keep my law. And you yourselves have done worse than your forefathers; for each of you follows the promptings of his wicked and stubborn heart instead of obeying me. So I will fling you headlong out of this land into a country unknown to you and to your forefathers; there you can serve other gods day and night, for I will show you no favour. (Jer. 16:11-13)

Today multitudes are frenetically seeking reality and meaning in the bland philosophies of oriental gurus, in the transcendentalism of mystical cults, in the psychedelic transports induced by exotic drugs, in the vapid prognostications of astrology and the empty consolations of spiritism, in the daring rituals of witchcraft and sorcery and even Satan worship, and in the superficial euphoria aroused by sanctimonious hucksters who demand ascetic discipline or encourage every kind of license — seeking and not finding, unless and until they turn to God for redemption and wholeness through Jesus Christ. Amidst the clamor and confusion of all the conflicting voices of our day it still remains true that "there is no salvation in anyone else at all, for there is no other name under heaven granted to men, by which we may receive salvation" (Acts 4:12). Any other remedy that is offered for the unrest of mankind is the spurious merchandise of those who belong to the line of deceivers and false prophets described by Paul as "enemies of the cross of Christ," whose "appetite is their god," who "glory in their shame," and who are "heading for destruction" (Phil. 3:18f.).

GOD'S RESTRAINING HAND

The image of God in man, however, has not been obliterated. It has been disfigured but not destroyed. This we must attribute to the controlling hand of God, who places restraints on the wickedness of man and the dehumanization of society. The reins are still in God's hands and it is due to the curb of his care that this world has not degenerated into an intolerable bedlam of hatred and a cesspool of vice. His image is discernible in the fact that happy interpersonal relations continue to be enjoyed in the community of the family group and of society in general; that, despite the crass irrationality of man's ungodliness and the many contradictions of his thought and conduct, he still has impressive powers of reason and intellect; that a concern for certain standards of decency and morality persists among men and that these standards commonly enjoy some measure of legislative protection; that crime and unruliness are ordinarily punished, indeed that police forces and law courts are established for the purpose of preserving order and protecting society from the evil in its midst; that much is being done, creatively, for the benefit of mankind through the progress of technological and medical science, and also in the sphere of literature and the arts by the production of works that are excellent and inspiring; and that, though millions are suffering harsh oppression, there are still many lands in which the basic freedoms of mankind are preserved and respected.

Man, in short, is still *God's* creature. He is part of the creation which God providentially sustains, and God will not allow his image in man to be extinguished. God has purposes for man, as for the rest of his creation, and those purposes cannot fail of fulfilment. As we shall see in the next chapter, the disintegrating effect of sin is counteracted by the reconciling work of Christ. We must emphasize again that the implications of the truth regarding man's creatureliness are of absolutely fundamental significance for man's understanding of himself and of his place and function within the whole scheme of creation. For man to refuse to acknowledge his creatureliness means that he does not begin to understand the true meaning of things. As man's being can be properly understood only in terms of the Creator-creature relationship, so the suppression of the truth concerning the Creator involves also the suppression of the truth concerning the creature. The ungodly man therefore cuts the very lifeline of his being. He brings upon himself sickness and death at the heart of his being because he sunders his constitution from the One of whom it is the image, and in relationship with whom the fulfilment of the amazing potential of his humanity can alone be achieved.

But the disorientation of man does not end with himself, for in falling away from God he has dragged down the rest of creation with him. This was only to be expected, since by his defiance of the Creator he has incapacitated himself as God's viceroy entrusted with the government of the earth. The confusion he has brought upon himself extends, through him, to the sphere of creation over which he was intended to exercise authority. The sickness of the head is communicated to the entire body. Thus the sin of man brings a curse upon the ground, with the result that every harvest is marred by the presence of thorns and thistles and the life of man becomes clouded with toil and sorrow and is cut short by death (Gen. 3:16ff.). "When thou dost rebuke a man to punish his sin," the Psalmist exclaims, "all his charm festers and drains away; indeed man is only a puff of wind" (Ps. 39:11). Paul writes of creation as having been made "the victim of frustration, not by its own choice," and as "groaning in all its parts" as it longingly awaits the universal restoration which will take place at Christ's appearing (Rom. 8:19ff.; cf. Acts 3:21); for if the fall of man has adversely affected the harmony of the whole, the rehabilitation of man will see the recovery of that concord between man and his Creator and between man and the world which was the mark of creation as it came from the hand of God, and the establishment of all that God purposed in his work as Creator. Meanwhile the earth labors under the crippling dislocations which have followed from the ungodliness of man.

THE TRUE IMAGE

We have attempted to show that the creation of man in the image of God is a fact of the most profound significance, but there is a further aspect of this doctrine which must now be briefly discussed. God, we are told, made man *in,* or *according to,* his own image (Gen. 1:27). This is not the same thing as saying that God made man *as* his own image, that the human creature *is* God's image — though in a general sense it is possible to speak in this way (see I Cor. 11:7). The description "the image of God" should be understood particularly as a reference to the Second Person of the Trinity, who as the eternal *Son* is also the eternal *likeness* of the Father. At the human level, a father is said to beget a son in his own likeness (cf. Gen. 5:3); but the human analogy, valuable though it is, is (like all human analogies) not fully competent to define the relationship between Father and Son within the mystery of the Godhead. In the case of man, there is identity of essence (humanness) but not union of being: a human father and his son are two separate entities. The Godhead is a unity, and eternally so, and in the mystery of the Trinity we may not conceive of the Father and the Son as separate individuals or entities. Accordingly, the Son is not described as being in or after or according to the image of the

Father: he *is* the likeness by whom God reveals himself. Being both God and Son he is "the stamp of God's very being" (Heb. 1:3).

The designation of the Son as the divine and eternal Word, or Logos (John 1:1ff.), has similar implications. At the human level, again, the word is the unit of rational communication and command, the revelation of the mind and the will of man. Unlike God's word, it is not infallible in its wisdom and in its power. He who is the eternal Word, however, perfectly reveals the mind of God and indefectibly enacts the will of God. This Word, moreover, is himself God, and as such he is not the revealer of someone other than himself, but is the self-revelation of God (cf. John 14:9). He is the creative Word through whom all things have come into being (John 1:3). He is the sustaining Word through whom all things are providentially kept in being (Heb. 1:3). He is the redeeming Word through whom the salvation of man and the world is effected (John 1:14). He is the judging Word through whom all ungodly opposition is finally quelled and righteousness and peace are established for ever (Rev. 19:11-16; cf. John 12:48). As the Word, therefore, who communicates the divine will, displays the divine mind, and executes the divine decree, the Son is the image of the Father.

These conclusions are confirmed by the manner in which the Son is explicitly described as "the very image of God" (II Cor. 4:4) and as "the image of the invisible God" (Col. 1:15), and by the doctrine that the redemption of man, by which the restoration of his creation in the image of God is achieved, brings about his transformation into the likeness of Christ, who is the true Image. Thus Paul teaches that Christians are being "transfigured into his image, from glory to glory" (II Cor. 3:18; cf. 4:4), that God has "ordained that they should be shaped to the image of his Son" (Rom. 8:29), and that man's new nature in Christ "is being constantly renewed in the image of its Creator" (Col. 3:10). This indicates that it has been God's purpose from the very beginning that man, whom he created in his own image, should be conformed to the likeness of him who is the Image, namely, the eternal Son. Christlikeness, in short, is the proper destiny of man. It is the purpose of his creation and the fulfilment of his humanity. Of this there will be more to say in the next chapter.

The reality of the divine image in which man was created, furthermore, has an important bearing on the question of the propriety and indeed the possibility of the incarnation. In the light of the absolute transcendence of the Creator and the finite insignificance of the creature, the notion of God becoming man, of the eternal Creator taking to himself the nature of his frail creature, seems to be highly incongruous. It certainly is something beyond human comprehension. That consideration, however, does not give man the right to dismiss the doctrine of the incarnation as an impossibility which is beyond belief. While the incarnation remains a mystery presented to Christian faith and proved by Christian experience, a clue to its appropriateness, and therefore to its "possibility," is provided by the understanding of man as created in the image of God. It is this fact which, as we have seen, renders man unique among all God's creatures. It indicates a special, though inexpressible, affinity between man and the eternal Son, who is himself the Image of God, and in whom accordingly man has been created. There is a nuclear point here, a dynamic potential, which affords man the capacity to be conformed to the Son, but which also, when man is in need of a redeemer, holds available the "possibility" for the Son to identify himself with man by becoming incarnate. In other words, between the Second Person of the Trinity and God's creature man there exists a mysterious bond which is the focal point of the divine purpose in creation, which will come to full expression when man at last is completely Christlike, and which, for the achievement of that end, "enables" the Son, without impropriety, to be born of Mary at Bethlehem in Judea as he takes to himself our human nature in order that he may redeem it. With this clue we may perhaps enter more fully into the meaning of the apostle when he declares that "God chose us in Christ before the world was founded, to be dedicated, to be without blemish in his sight," and that "in his love he destined us — such was his will and pleasure — to be accepted as his sons through Jesus Christ." Indeed, it has always been God's intention that his purposes for the whole of creation should come to fulfilment *in Christ,* for God, says Paul, "has made known to us his hidden purpose — such was his will and pleasure determined beforehand in Christ — to be put into effect when the time was ripe: namely, that the universe, all in heaven and on earth, might be brought into a unity in Christ" (Eph. 1:4f., 9f.).

Not without justification was man described long ago as *the image of the Image.* In Christ man attains his destiny of conformity to that Image.

they are caused by the alienation of the creature from the Creator. If alienation is the bane of the world, reconciliation is its cure and its blessing.

This decisive intervention for our everlasting redemption was achieved through the incarnation, the becoming man, of the eternal Son, who, as John says, "became flesh and dwelt among us" (John 1:14). The logic of the incarnation and the manner in which it served God's purpose of redemption will be considered in this chapter. First, however, we must return to the question of the "possibility" of the assumption of our humanity by him who is neither a creature nor a human being but the divine Son through whom all things were created. The solution to this question is to be sought, as has been suggested, in the understanding that the Son, who in his eternal being is the Image of God, is also therefore the image in or after whom man was originally created. Thus a certain mysterious affinity between mankind and the Second Person of the Trinity is indicated. The attainment of perfect conformity to him who is the True Image is man's full glory and his intended destiny. The tragedy of man is his willful failure to maintain this unique dignity of his creation, displayed in his contempt for the divine image which is constitutive of his self-fulfilment as the chief of all God's creatures. The becoming man of him who is the Image after which man was created is, so to speak, a "possibility" inherent in this special relationship — a "possibility" which is always there, a potential available and ready at hand, as it were. Human language is not competent to speak with any adequacy of such a mystery, but we may at least venture to draw this conclusion: that God was by no means unprepared for the eventuality of the fall of man; he was not taken by surprise and, manlike, forced to devise in a makeshift manner an emergency plan for the rehabilitation of his wayward creatures. The means of restoration was there at hand, "built in" from the very beginning. God, in the person of the Image, was fully equipped to take action on behalf of mankind created in the Image. The Image himself intervenes to the end that man may recover his true likeness by attaining conformity to that Image which is essential to the fullness of his being.

It might be argued that God could justly have destroyed his creatures because of their ungodliness, but then the problem would arise that for him to annihilate sinful mankind whom he originally formed in his own image would be incongruous and self-defeating. It would mean the failure of his work of creation, and that in turn would mean the contradiction involved in his failure as God. "What, then, was God to do?" asks Athanasius; and he replies:

> What else could be done, than for him to renew his image in mankind, so that through it men might once more be able to know him? And how could this be done save by the coming of the very Image of God himself, our Saviour Jesus Christ? Men could not have done it, since they are only made after the Image; nor could angels have done it, for they are not the images of God. Therefore the Word of God came in his own person, so that he, as the Image of the Father, might create man anew after the Image.[1]

Thus, in the incarnation, he who is the Image after which man was made becomes man in order that he may restore the perfection of that image which man by his sinfulness has defaced. The destiny of man is realized through the incarnate Son's identification of himself with our humanity, by his purification of our humanity, and by his exaltation of our humanity, in and with himself, to that state of glorification for which it was always intended.

Where mankind failed in Adam mankind succeeds in

---

1. Athanasius, *The Incarnation of the Word of God,* § 13.

Christ. What man lost through Adam's fall is regained through Christ's victory. Indeed, far more is won for man in Christ than was forfeited in Adam. Thus Paul writes:

> God's act of grace is out of all proportion to Adam's wrongdoing. For if the wrongdoing of that one man brought death upon so many, its effect is vastly exceeded by the grace of God and the gift that came to so many by that one man, Jesus Christ . . . . For if by the wrongdoing of that one man death established its reign, through a single sinner, much more shall those who receive in far greater measure God's grace, and his gift of righteousness, live and reign through the one man, Jesus Christ. (Rom. 5:15-17)

Accordingly, in comparison with Adam, the first man, made of dust, Paul describes the incarnate Son as "the last Adam," "the second man," and " the heavenly man," and says that the destiny of redeemed mankind is to "wear the image of the heavenly man" (I Cor. 15:45-49). In Christ, the last Adam, the human race not only makes a fresh start but also now, in the place of failure and defeat, overcomes, thanks to the perfect obedience of the Second Man, and is assured of reaching the glorious goal of conformity to the heavenly Image which was set before the first Adam, but which he failed to reach because of his disobedience.

THE TRUE DESTINY OF MAN

The "possibility" of the incarnation resides, then, in the existence of a particular though mysterious affinity between man, who has been created in the image of God, and the eternal Son, who himself is that Image. Thus the incarnation is specifically the incarnation of the Second Person of the Trinitarian Godhead — not of the Father or of the Holy Spirit, but of the Son. The theme of the purpose or design of the incarnation, and the logic of it, is strikingly developed by the author of the Epistle to the Hebrews. It is significant that he takes his lead from Psalm 8, which is not, on the face of it, messianic in character, but an ode on the greatness of the Creator and the contrast between man's insignificance, on the one hand, and his dignity, on the other, within the majestic range of God's creation. Made lower than the angels, though only "for a short while," since his destiny is, by attainment to the fulness of that Image in which he has been created, to be exalted to a position higher than the angels, man was in a position in which he was "crowned with glory and honour." God set him over the works of his hands and "put all things in subjection under his feet." Man, however, has not been faithful to his trust. He has not dutifully carried out the mandate committed to him as God's viceroy on earth, with the result that human society together with the rest of creation where man touches it is marred by discord and dislocation. Such being the case, the regrettable reality of the human situation is that "we do not yet see all things in subjection to man" (Heb. 2:5-8).

But we do see Jesus, "who for a short while was made lower than the angels, crowned now with glory and honour." In other words, the Psalmist's theme which failed of fulfilment in man has found fulfilment in Jesus, the incarnate Son. In him who became the Son of Man the true destiny of man is achieved. He is the Second Man, whose will was one with the divine will, and in whom accordingly the true humanness of God's creature man is at last realized. It is important to notice that the writer of Hebrews is speaking of *Jesus,* that is to say, the incarnate Son, our fellow man. By becoming the Son of Man (without of course ceasing to be the Son of God, for he is God doing all this for us), he, the Image in which we were created, has united our humanity to himself and thereby has assured us that he "does not shrink from calling men his brothers" (Heb. 2:9-11).

The chief intention of the incarnation, as Athanasius observes with reference to this passage in Hebrews, was "that the Word might take to himself a body for the purpose of offering it in sacrifice for other like bodies."[2] He became man in order that as Man he might die for man. Thus the author of Hebrews insists that his being made lower than the angels for a short while was "so that, by God's gracious will, in tasting death he should stand for us all." Again, he shared our flesh and blood for this reason, "that through death he might break the power of him who had death at his command, that is, the devil, and might liberate those who, through fear of death, had all their lifetime been in servitude" (Heb. 2:9, 14f.). Furthermore, by his resurrection and exaltation he has raised and exalted our humanity, the humanity he, as the incarnate Son, has made his own, to the glorious height, above all angels, for which it was always destined. It is of this great truth that Paul is speaking when he extols the mighty power God exerted in Christ

> when he raised him from the dead, when he enthroned him at his right hand in the heavenly realms, far above all government and authority, all power and dominion, and any title of sovereignty that can be named, not only in this age but in the age to come, and when he put everything in subjection under his feet.

Precisely this same mighty power, Paul goes on to explain, is active in the life of the Christian believer:

> God, rich in mercy, for the great love he bore us, brought us to life with Christ even when we were dead in our sins; it is by his grace you are saved. And in union with Christ Jesus he raised us up and enthroned us with him in the heavenly realms. (Eph. 1:19ff.; 2:4ff.)

We see, then, that the destiny of the incarnate Son is at

---

2. Athanasius, *The Incarnation of the Word of God,* § 10.

the same time the destiny of our humanity which he has taken to himself. It is in Christ, accordingly, that the divine purpose of creation, as summarized in Psalm 8, is accomplished — the purpose, namely, of crowning man with glory and honor and of establishing the order and harmony of the whole of creation under the governance of man conformed to the divine Image in which he was made. Redemption in Christ achieves the goal of creation in the Image, for through him the renewal of all things becomes an endless reality (cf. II Cor. 5:17; II Peter 3:13; Rev. 21:1-5).

We must now inquire more precisely into the method by which this goal is brought to fulfilment, and into the logic that lies behind this method. We have considered, so far, how the key to the "possibility" of the incarnation is to be sought in the mysterious truth that the Son himself is the Image in which man was created, and how the object of the incarnation was his complete identification with our humanity to the end that he might offer himself up in our place, Brother for brother, so to speak (cf. Heb. 2:11). The place of his self-offering was the hill of Calvary where he died, like a criminal, on a cross.

THE PERFECT OBEDIENCE OF CHRIST

The death of Christ would have been unavailing, however, had it not been preceded by a life that was entirely pure and blameless. It was essential for him first to establish his perfection as our fellow man by meeting and overcoming every kind of trial to which mankind is prone. Hence the special significance of his temptation in the wilderness, when the devil, in direct confrontation, endeavored to destroy his personal integrity and thereby to frustrate the purpose of his coming into the world. The devil did not succeed then, nor did he succeed in any of the other temptations by which the incarnate Son was daily assailed. This is what the author of the Epistle to the Hebrews is speaking of when he asserts that the captain of our salvation was "made perfect through sufferings" (Heb. 2:10). This perfection of Jesus was not something static, a mere "state," but something achieved, actively, through his constant and unyielding conquest of evil. For him to have failed at any point would have meant his lapsing from perfection to imperfection, his imitation of the sorry history of the first man, and would at once have disqualified him from serving as the sinner's savior on the cross. Indeed, so far from being a savior, he himself would then have been in need of a savior, for he would have forfeited the unblemished integrity of his humanity. He would have failed in his purpose of being man as God intended him to be, living his life in total obedience to the divine will, and thus realizing the full potential of his (and therefore our) manhood. It is of the greatest importance, then, that he was "tested in every way, as we are, only without sin" (Heb. 4:15), that it was meat and drink to him always and only to do the Father's will and to finish the work committed to him (John 4:34), and that as he faced the supreme ordeal of the cross he could declare, "I have glorified thee on earth by completing the work which thou gavest me to do" (John 17:4).

Under the Old Testament system it was a requirement that animals offered in sacrifice should be free of all physical defect. In this way the need for a truly spotless victim to be slain in the stead of sinful man was typified. These ancient sacrifices could not achieve atonement and reconciliation for man, because a *morally* spotless victim was required to effect this purpose. A dumb, irrational, uncomprehending beast is not a creature morally responsible before God, for it has not been made "in the Image," and therefore it can never be a fitting substitute for man. But the incarnate Son, by reason of the genuineness of the manhood he has assumed, and, what is more, by reason of the perfection of that manhood established by the total grace and goodness of his life and by his victory over every temptation, offered himself up as a true substitute for the sinner. He proved himself to be what man had failed to reflect, the Image without fault. Thus Peter explains that it is not with perishable things, like gold or silver, that we have been redeemed: "The price was paid in precious blood, blood as it were of a lamb without mark or blemish — the blood of Christ . . . . For Christ died for our sins once and for all. He, the just, suffered for the unjust, to bring us to God" (I Peter 1:18f.; 3:18). At the cross he took the sinner's place, the innocent for the guilty, the holy for the unholy. In him at last we see the true substitution: Man for man. In the words of Newman's hymn, at Calvary God "smote in Man for man the foe":

> O loving wisdom of our God!
>   When all was sin and shame,
> A second Adam to the fight
>   And to the rescue came.
>
> O wisest love! that flesh and blood,
>   Which did in Adam fail,
> Should strive afresh against the foe,
>   Should strive and should prevail.

THE MANNER OF CHRIST'S DYING

By his incarnation, then, the Son became fully qualified to stand in the place of man, and this he did when he offered up himself as a holy and spotless victim on the cross. Moreover, the *manner* of his dying, that is, on a cross, has its own particular significance. For him to have died of disease or of old age, or to have perished at the hand of an assassin, would not have sufficed. It was necessary that he should die, and be seen to die, as a criminal, judicially condemned to suffer the ignominious execution reserved for the basest of malefactors (cf. Mark 10:32-34). At the same time it was necessary that this should be seen to be the condemnation of an innocent person, that the spectacle of the cross of Calvary should manifestly be that of the innocent suffering and dying for the guilty. This was dramatically confirmed by the fact that when Jesus was executed he was nailed to a cross which had been prepared for someone else: he actually took the place of Barabbas, a common criminal convicted of sedition and murder (Mark 15:7ff.). Apart from the consideration that the guiltlessness, indeed the absolute goodness, of Jesus was well known to all who demanded his execution, he was also repeatedly declared innocent of offense by the Roman judge who presided at his trial and who yet handed him over to be crucified (Luke 23:4, 14, 22ff.). At the human level, therefore, there was a gross and deliberate miscarriage of justice which was plain for all to see. Jesus, furthermore, not only took the place of the evildoer; he also took his place with the evildoers, one of whom was crucified on either side of him. His identification of himself with our sinful humanity could not have been more graphically demonstrated. And so it was that the ancient prophecy of Isaiah received its fulfilment:

> He was despised and rejected by men,
> tormented and humbled by suffering . . . .
> Yet on himself he bore our sufferings,
> our torments he endured . . . .
> But he was pierced for our transgressions,
> tortured for our iniquities;

the chastisement he bore is health for us
and by his scourging we are healed . . . .
The Lord laid on him the guilt of us all . . . .
He was reckoned among transgressors,
because he bore the sin of many
and interceded for their transgressions. (Isa. 53:3-6, 12)

The death of the incarnate Son as the world's sin-bearer was indeed unique. By virtue of that death he has become the sole mediator between God and men (I Tim. 2:5). Consequently, as Peter proclaimed, "there is no salvation in anyone else at all, for there is no other name under heaven granted to men, by which we may receive salvation" (Acts 4:12). It was not, however, merely the physical sufferings of Christ that were unique. Many others have resolutely endured gross injustice, savage cruelty, and excruciating pain in dying. The uniqueness of Christ's suffering lies, rather, in its moral and spiritual character. This is glimpsed in the agony of Gethsemane which preceded the agony of the cross. The ordeal through which the incarnate Son passed was nothing less than the horror of hell, the hell due to us, the taking upon himself of all the guilt and vileness of the world's sin, our sin, the exhausting in his own holy person of the judgment of God against the ungodly wickedness of man. Smitten with the rod of divine wrath in our stead he enters into the dark abyss of abandonment which wrings from him the cry of dereliction: "My God, my God, why hast thou forsaken me?" (Mark 15:34). This is the hour of God's dealing with the evil which is at the root of all man's problems, the hour when our Brother, the Second Man, experienced to the full for our sakes the chaotic irrationality, the blank lostness and alienation, the severing of the lifeline, and the dread depth of desolation which are the consequences of human sinfulness. It is the hour when he who was innocent of sin took to himself the punishment of our sin so that, by a gracious exchange, we might take to ourselves the perfection of his righteousness and in him be acceptable to God (cf. II Cor. 5:21).

GOD IN ACTION

In all that took place at this crucial hour there is a complete harmony between the Father and the Son, for it is the one God who, by way of the incarnation and the cross, is acting decisively for our redemption. From beginning to end it is God's action for the reconciliation of the world to himself (II Cor. 5:18f.). There can be no question, therefore, of any kind of division or contrariety within the Godhead, as though the Father were angry and the Son well-disposed towards us, or as though the Son had by the desperate resort of his self-offering to bring about a change in the Father's attitude. The initiative of redemption all along is God's initiative, and the impulse is the impulse of his love. It is because God so *loved* the world that he gave his only Son (John 3:16). God, indeed, is love, "and his love was disclosed to us in this," and precisely in this, "that he sent his only Son into the world to bring us life" (I John 4:9).

At the same time, it is true, the cross makes plain the awful seriousness of sin and its consequences. To disregard unrighteousness within his creation would make nonsense of the justice and holiness of God and would undermine the moral structure of the world. To act thus might be sentimental, but it would hardly be loving. Sin must be treated as sin, and it can be dealt with only by meeting and absorbing its wage, namely, death (Rom. 6:23). At Calvary, accordingly, we witness not only the triumph of God's love, but its triumph through the satisfaction of his justice. It is on the basis of the satisfaction of divine justice that the sinner is justified (cf. Rom. 3:21-26). The love of God and the justice of God belong together; they are the two sides of the same coin. They are not two irreconcilable opposites. If the cross is not a place of justice it is not a place of love. Divorced from justice, what took place at Calvary would be a demonstration of needless cruelty rather than of sovereign love. Only against the dark background of the holy judgment of God against sin does the loving light of the cross shine forth with its full intensity. The wonder of the cross is that there God himself graciously meets the demands of his own holiness on behalf of his sinful creatures, that there, out of pure love, he absorbs, as the incarnate Son, his own wrath against our sin by himself enduring the punishment due to us.

We must resist the temptation to sentimentalize the cross. To transmute it into a jeweled ornament is not to enhance it; it is, rather, to obscure its evangelical meaning. The cross is a gibbet, the gruesome instrument of the most shameful of deaths. Properly viewed, it should convince us of the enormity of our sin and of the infinite costliness, to God, of our redemption. It is an object as ghastly as our sin is foul and defiling and dishonoring to the goodness of our holy Creator. The cross, indeed, is the means of our blessing, but it is itself accursed. Nailed to it, the incarnate Son identified himself with the curse that man's sin brought upon the world — a curse which involved sorrow and sweat, thorns and death (Gen. 3:16ff.). So deep was the Son's humiliation of himself that he became the man of sorrows, crowned not with gold but with thorns, the sweat of his agony great drops of blood (Luke 22:44), and his death that of the abhorred outcast from human society. Paul writes, "Christ brought us freedom from the curse of the law by becoming for our sake an accursed thing; for Scripture says, 'A curse is on everyone who is hanged on a gibbet' " (Gal. 3:13; cf. Deut. 21:23).

Inevitably, the cross is the great dividing place for mankind. To turn away from the blessing that flows from it is to continue under the curse. Those who reject the grace of God receive the judgment of God; they love darkness rather than light; they choose death instead of life (John 3:19f.). By that same cross each of us is either saved or judged. This truth is well exemplified by the presence of the two malefactors on either side of the cross of Christ. Each is in a situation of desperate need. One repents and calls on the dying Savior for mercy; the other brazenly treats him with mockery and contempt. The death of one is lit up by faith and the promise of immediate blessing; the other dies in the bitter darkness of his impenitence and unbelief (Luke 23:39ff.). These two malefactors are a picture of all mankind, divided by the cross of Christ into faith and unbelief. At the cross the repentant sinner finds grace and forgiveness, but at the same cross the unrepentant sinner stands judged and condemned. Certainly, the primary purpose of the cross is the salvation of mankind; but when the grace of God that flows from it is spurned it becomes the instrument of condemnation. The truth in fact is simply this: that he who rejects its grace stands self-condemned before his Creator.

THE SOVEREIGNTY OF GOD

Now the question arises as to the ultimate effectiveness of what God has done for us in Christ. Granted that, being *God's* action, the saving work of Christ is fully adequate for the forgiveness of all sin and the restoration of true harmony between man and his Maker; yet the possibility of our turning away from the grace of redemption would seem to carry with it the possibility of there being no positive response at all to that grace, in which case the incarnation and the cross would in the end have proved completely vain and fruitless. Fortunately, it may be said, things have turned out otherwise and this has proved to be no more than an extreme and hypothetical possibility — after all there is the historical phenomenon of the Christian church! Yet, even so, God would still be left in a state of uncertainty regarding the ultimate measure of success or failure of his saving operation. We must resist the temptation to reduce God to the proportions of a being who is subject to the restrictions and frustrations of our human existence. To do so is both unwise and unrealistic. We are speaking of God, not man, of him who is infinite, not finite. We should accept it as absolutely certain, therefore, that the redeeming work of God in Christ cannot fail to achieve the purpose for which it was performed, namely, the salvation of the world. The incarnation was not a gamble on God's part. It was a definite means to a predetermined end. God's word never returns to him fruitless but always accomplishes what he has purposed (Isa. 55:11): how can this fail to be true in particular of him who is personally and supremely the Word of God (John 1:1ff.)? What God intends he fulfils. If his purposes in creation cannot fail, this is no less true of his purposes in redemption — indeed, as has already been explained, it is through his work of redemption that his work of creation achieves its goal: creation and redemption belong within the same perspective of the divine will.

In other words, God sovereignly governs all things in accordance with the purpose of his will. And this is the significance of the doctrine of divine *election* (cf. Eph. 1:4f.). All, once again, is of God, who not only begins but also completes what he begins, whether it be his work in redemption (Phil. 1:6) or his work in creation (Rev. 21:1ff.). God's election, it must be stressed, remains a *mystery, his* mystery: it is not a simple matter of elementary arithmetic, however much we might like to make it so. A divine mystery is not there to be solved by reducing it to a human equation. God's election is his assurance to us that his work of grace in Christ Jesus will not be unfruitful, that the end for which it was designed will certainly be attained; and it assures us, further, that all is of divine grace, that we owe our enjoyment of redemption entirely to the prior goodness of God. Thus Paul insists that it is by God's grace that we are saved, through faith, and that it is not at all our doing: "It is God's gift, not a reward for work done. There is nothing for anyone to boast of. For we are God's handiwork" (Eph. 2:8-10). The initiative and the power belong solely to God: "For at the very time when we were still powerless, then Christ died for the wicked . . . . Christ died for us while we were yet sinners, and that is God's own proof of his love towards us" (Rom. 5:6, 8). God came to our aid when we were quite unable to help ourselves. Therefore all the glory is his, and everyone who is reborn in Christ is constrained to acknowledge with Paul: "By God's grace I am what I am" (I Cor. 15:10). And we should notice that the apostle immediately adds that God's bestowal of grace on him was "not in vain," for *God's* activity is never in vain.

This, too, is the confident assurance of the incarnate Son who came into the world to save sinners (I Tim. 1:15). He knows that his work will unfailingly result in the salvation of sinners precisely because he knows that all whom the Father gives him will come to him and that of these he will lose not even one (John 6:37-39). Even the power to come to him is due to the enabling grace of God. That is why Jesus adds:

"No man can come to me unless he is drawn by the Father who sent me" (John 6:44). God's work of redemption, accordingly, simply because it is *God's* work, is infallibly effective. This means, further, that the believer's security in Christ is an *eternal* security. A salvation that was insecure, or that could be lost, would not only in itself be contradictory but would also stamp the saving action of God with uncertainty, thus reducing it to the level of human action, and that, as we have seen, would be intolerable. The eternal life which is promised and given in Christ would not be eternal if it could cease or be lost (John 3:16, etc.). The Good Shepherd, however, gives this guarantee: "My own sheep listen to my voice; I know them and they follow me. I give them eternal life and they shall never perish; no one shall snatch them from my care" (John 10:27).

THE RESPONSIBILITY OF MAN

But the mystery of divine election does not eliminate our own responsibility before God. The very fact that we are God's creatures made in his image means, as we have seen, that we are answerable to him. When God addresses us with the message of the gospel he addresses us as sinful beings, indeed, but none the less as responsible beings. The very fact of our responsibility implies that the seat of sin and ungodliness within us is not so much in the intellect and the emotions as in the will. The sinner's attitude is one of obstinate rebellion, while the believer willingly turns to God in penitence and trust as he accepts the grace freely offered him in Christ. Not only did Jesus proclaim, "The man who comes to me I will never turn away" (John 6:37), and extend to his hearers the invitation, "If anyone is thirsty let him come to me" (John

7:37), but he also reproved those who persisted in their un-belief with the words, "You refuse to come to me that you may have life" (John 5:40), and solemnly warned, "If you do not believe that I am what I am, you will die in your sins" (John 8:24). That divine election and human responsibility are not incompatible with each other is apparent, for exam-ple, in the Epistle to the Romans where, in the midst of a famous passage on the subject of election, Paul affirms that "there is no distinction between Jew and Greek [that is, all men no matter how they may be classified], because the same Lord is Lord of all, and is rich enough for the need of all who call upon him; for 'everyone who calls upon the name of the Lord will be saved.' " And this consideration is the ground of the necessity for the universal proclamation of the gospel:

> How could they call on one in whom they had no faith? And how could they have faith in one they had never heard of? And how could they hear without someone to spread the news? And how could anyone spread the news unless he had been sent to do so? And that is what Scripture affirms: "How welcome are the feet of the messengers of good news!" (Rom. 10:12-15; cf. Isa. 52:7)

Universal responsibility requires universal evangelism. The proclamation of the gospel in turn demands, and always receives, a response, whether positive or negative. The declaration, "To you the message of this salvation has been sent," is at the same time the challenge to repent and trust in him through whom "forgiveness of sins is preached to you" (Acts 13:26, 38). To reject the gospel is to be self-con-demned; it is to choose the judgment of God instead of the mercy of God. This is clearly stated in the words of Jesus to Nicodemus: "The man who puts his faith in the Son does not come under judgment; but the unbeliever has already been judged in that he has not given his allegiance to God's only Son" (John 3:18).

THE PERIL OF SELF-RIGHTEOUSNESS

The position of the unbeliever is essentially that of self-righteousness: maintaining that he is righteous in himself, he is unwilling to acknowledge himself a sinner and unable to admit his need of God's justifying righteousness which is freely offered him in Christ. Self-righteousness is thus the greatest hindrance to the acceptance of the gospel, and it is particularly reprehensible in the case of the person who is preoccupied with being religious and who imagines that God must be favorably impressed with his religiousness. At heart, in fact, self-righteousness is irreligious, for it is thoroughly self-centered rather than God-centered. The sternest censures of Jesus were reserved for the proudly religious and vainly self-righteous Pharisees (see Matt. 23). The parable of the Pharisee and the tax-collector (Luke 18:9ff.) is a condemnation of those "who are sure of their own goodness [KJV, "who trust in themselves that they are righteous"] and look down on everyone else," and a declaration that the forgiving grace of God is granted only to those who humbly acknowledge their sinfulness and call upon him for mercy. How could it be otherwise, since it is sinners that Christ came to save (Mark 2:17; I Tim. 1:15)? The self-righteous man blinds himself to his own sinfulness. In his self-esteem he sees no need of grace and mercy; and so, by his very self-righteousness, he actually excludes himself from the grace of the gospel. Self-righteousness, therefore, and not least within the church, is the enemy of the gospel. It knows no need of the gospel for itself and it has no message of the gospel for others.

Fortunately, it is possible for self-adequacy to come to the end of itself and thereby to come to the beginning of the experience of redemption; that is, to acknowledge what one truly is, a sinner, guilty and unworthy before God. The road to the truth leads from self-centeredness to God-centeredness, and Jesus Christ himself is the way (John 14:6). This is the lesson which that super-religious, self-righteous Pharisee Saul of Tarsus had to learn. Filled with indignant hostility, he had treated Jesus and his gospel with "abuse and persecution and outrage"; but, he testifies, "I was dealt with mercifully," for "the grace of our Lord was lavished upon me, with the faith and love which are ours in Christ Jesus" (I Tim. 1:13f.). Abandoning the rags of his self-righteousness (cf. Isa. 64:6), he clothed his sinful self with the perfect righteousness of the incarnate Son (cf. Rom. 13:12, 14; Gal. 3:27; Rev. 7:9) and was given his place in the eternal purposes of God as Paul the apostle of Jesus Christ (cf. Acts 26:16ff.; I Cor. 1:1, etc.). From then on the only righteousness that had any meaning for him was righteousness-in-Christ. Thus he writes to the members of the Philippian church:

> What things were gain to me, those I counted loss for Christ. Yea doubtless, and I count all things but loss for the excellency of the knowledge of Christ Jesus my Lord, for whom I have suffered the loss of all things, and do count them but dung, that I may win Christ, and be found in him, not having mine own righteousness, which is of the law, but that which is through the faith of Christ, the righteousness which is of God by faith. (Phil. 3:7-9, KJV)

Paul never ceased to thank God that, although he had so savagely persecuted the church, he had been made a recipient of his electing grace and thus had been brought into a vital involvement in the eternal purposes of his Creator. "In his good pleasure," he says, "God, who had set me apart from birth and called me through his grace, chose to reveal his Son to me and through me, in order that I might proclaim him among the Gentiles'' (Gal. 1:13-16). With this knowledge, he could never doubt the sovereign goodness of God or the unfailing effectiveness of his will. What the incarnate Son said to his apostles he says to all whom he calls to follow him: "You did not choose me: I chose you. I appointed you to go and bear fruit, fruit that shall last" (John 15:16). The fact that many because of their foolish self-centeredness exclude themselves from the "great banquet" to which God invites them does not mean that there will be empty seats at God's board. It is precisely those who have a sense of their need who are brought in, indeed who are *compelled* to come in (Luke 14:16-24). There are some who stumble at the notion of God's using compulsion to bring men and women into his kingdom; but God's compulsion is not the compulsion of a tyrant, but the compulsion of his boundless mercy and goodness. To be "compelled" to enter into the enjoyment of the divine hospitality in Christ Jesus is not grievous. That *force majeure* which restores our shattered relationship with our Creator and thus gives us back the fulness of our humanity is no violation of our rights. C. S. Lewis experienced and was grateful for the divine compulsion:

> You must picture me alone in that room at Magdalen, night after night, feeling, whenever my mind lifted even for a second from my work, the steady, unrelenting approach of Him whom I so earnestly desired not to meet. That which I greatly feared had at last come upon me. In the Trinity Term of 1929 I gave in, and admitted that God was God, and knelt and prayed . . . . The words *compelle intrare,* compel them to come in, have been so abused by wicked men that we shudder at them; but, properly understood, they plumb the depth of the Divine mercy. The hardness of God is kinder than the softness of men, and His compulsion is our liberation.[3]

---

3. C. S. Lewis, *Surprised by Joy,* pp. 182f.

The poet Francis Thompson speaks of the same divine insistence in "The Hound of Heaven":

> I fled Him down the nights and down the days;
> I fled Him down the arches of the years;
> I fled Him down the labyrinthine ways
>   Of my own mind; and in the midst of tears
> I hid from Him, and under running laughter.
>   Up vistaed hopes I sped;
>   And shot, precipitated,
> Adown Titanic glooms of chasmèd fears,
> From those strong Feet that followed, followed after.
>   But with unhurrying chase,
>   And unperturbèd pace,
> Deliberate speed, majestic instancy,
>   They beat — and a Voice beat
>   More instant than the Feet —
> "All things betray thee, who betrayest Me . . . .
> Naught shelters thee, who wilt not shelter Me . . . .
> Lo! naught contents thee, who content'st not Me . . . .
> Lo, all things fly thee, for thou fliest Me! . . .
> Alack, thou knowest not
> How little worthy of any love thou art!
> Whom wilt thou find to love ignoble thee
>   Save Me, save only Me?
> All which I took from thee I did but take
>   Not for thy harms,
> But just that thou might'st seek it in My arms.
>   All which thy child's mistake
> Fancies as lost, I have stored for thee at home:
>   Rise, clasp My hand, and come!"
>
>   Halts by me that footfall:
>   Is my gloom, after all,
> Shade of His hand, outstretched caressingly?
>   "Ah, fondest, blindest, weakest,
>   I am He Whom thou seekest!
> Thou dravest love from thee, who dravest Me."

ELECTION IN CHRIST

In speaking of divine election it is important to notice that the election of the believer takes place *in Christ,* who both enacts and mediates redemptive grace. There is no election apart from or outside of Christ, for he himself is in a unique sense the Elect of God. He alone is God's Chosen One (Isa. 42:1). Thus on the mount of transfiguration the voice from heaven declares: "This is my Son, my Chosen" (Luke 9:35); and Peter says of him: "Predestined before the foundation of the world, he was made manifest in this last period of time for your sake" (I Peter 1:20). It follows that our election or chosenness is not in ourselves but only in him. Only as, by God's grace, we become one with him through faith do we participate in the chosenness of him who is well-pleasing to God. This does not at all imply that our election is dependent on us, for that would make nonsense of the whole concept of election. It is God, not we, who does the electing in accordance with his antecedent purposes. "In Christ he chose us before the world was founded, to be dedicated, to be without blemish in his sight, to be full of love; and he destined us — such is his will and pleasure — to be accepted as his sons through Jesus Christ" (Eph. 1:4f.). The destiny of redeemed humanity, once again, is one with the destiny of Jesus Christ who, as the incarnate Son, is the Second Man.

Paradoxically — that is, in a manner contrary to what seems to be the case — it is in the suffering and death of the incarnate Son at Calvary that we have the most striking example of God's sovereign control over all that takes place. If there is anything in human history that should teach us not to judge solely by appearances, it is the cross of Jesus. There, it is true, we see the greatest concentration of the forces of evil that has ever been seen. At Calvary we are in the presence of the greatest wickedness and injustice in the whole of history. In the condemnation and crucifixion of Jesus evil seemed to have triumphed decisively over all that is good and pure and holy. The death of Jesus and the placing of his corpse in a tomb seemed only to mean the defeat of Jesus, the conquest of light by darkness, the annihilation of life by death. Jesus himself called it "the hour when darkness reigns" (Luke 22:53), and such it certainly was, for in that hour the power of evil vented its full rage and fury against God and his holy will. It was the dark hour when the Son of Man was betrayed into the hands of sinful men (Mark 14:41).

Yet it was also and particularly *Jesus'* hour, for it was the very hour for which he had come into the world (John 12:27): Calvary is the purpose and the explanation of Bethlehem. He came to save, and to save by dying, and by dying on the cross (Mark 10:45; John 12:31-33; I Tim. 1:15). Accordingly, Jesus embraced it, not as the hour of disaster, but as the hour of fulfilment, so much so that he described it as "the hour for the Son of Man to be glorified" (John 12:33)! At the time, indeed, it did not seem to his followers to be such. They saw clearly enough the hand of evil at work, but they failed to see that God's almighty hand was also at work in the terrible things they witnessed; and when their Master's body was laid lifeless in the tomb all that they had hoped and believed seemed to be irretrievably shattered and they were overwhelmed with gloom and despair. No doubt, they should have known that God was majestically in control of all that was taking place, for their Master had carefully and repeatedly told them that the road to Jerusalem would be for him the road of rejection and death — and also resurrection (Matt. 16:21ff.; 17:22f.; 20:17ff.; Mark 8:31ff.; 9:31f.; 10:32ff.; Luke 9:22; 18:31ff.).But it was only afterwards, when the risen Lord showed himself to them in person, and when the ascended Master sent them the promised Holy Spirit, that they fully understood that at Calvary the victory was God's and not Satan's.

After his resurrection Jesus took special care to explain to his disciples how in his suffering and death, and in the victory of his resurrection, the scriptures of the Old Testament were fulfilled. He chided the two disciples on the road to Emmaus for being "slow to believe all that the prophets said. Was the Messiah not bound to suffer thus before entering upon his glory?" he asked. And "then he began with Moses and all the prophets and explained to them the passages which referred to himself in every part of the scriptures" (Luke 24:25-27). Thereafter he appeared to his apostles, who had not yet grasped the reality of his resurrection, and reassured his wondering listeners with these words: "This is what I meant by saying, while I was still with you, that everything written about me in the Law of Moses and in the prophets and psalms was bound to be fulfilled." So, the account continues, "he opened their minds to understand the scriptures," concluding with this affirmation: "This is what is written: that the Messiah is to suffer death and to rise from the dead on the third day, and that in his name repentance bringing the forgiveness of sins is to be proclaimed to all nations" (Luke 24:44-47).

GOD IN CONTROL

The incarnate Son therefore went to suffer and die in

Jerusalem deliberately and of set purpose, in accordance with the divinely ordained plan for the world's salvation. He was in control of the situation all along, and even when he was seized by hostile hands and mocked and scourged and spat upon, and finally nailed in seemingly complete helplessness to the shameful cross, it was he who permitted this to be done to him. His submission to the malice of those who tormented him and did him to death was still his action. At the same time the part of those who wickedly treated him in this way was still their action. At Calvary the powers of love and light on the one hand and of hatred and darkness on the other met head-on in crucial conflict. Behind what the human eye saw, which was a helpless figure dying on a cross, was the sovereign, though unseen, purpose and control of Almighty God. It was not the helplessness of God but the will of God that was witnessed there. Thus Jesus said to Peter when he drew his sword to defend his Master at the moment of his arrest: "Put up your sword . . . . Do you suppose that I cannot appeal to my Father, who would at once send to my aid more than twelve legions of angels?" (Matt. 26:52f.). To Pilate's question, "Surely you know that I have authority to release you, and I have authority to crucify you?" Jesus replied, "You would have no authority at all over me, if it had not been granted you from above" (John 19:10f.). And earlier he had told his disciples, when speaking to them as the Good Shepherd: "I lay down my life for the sheep . . . . No one has robbed me of it; I am laying it down of my own free will. I have the power to lay it down, and I have the power to take it again" (John 10:15-18).

For him who had given evidence of his sovereign lordship by his stilling of the unruly elements, his feeding of the multitude, his healing of the sick and afflicted, and indeed his raising of the dead — not to mention the pure goodness of his person and the sublime content of his teaching — the cross, loathed by all, was the experience of deepest humiliation. It was humiliation, certainly, at the hands of those who persecuted him with such malice; but it was none the less *self*-humiliation, for it was none other than the incarnate Son, the raiser of the dead, who was himself now passing through the dark experience of death. How strange, this passion of him who is the Lord of Life! How could it be other than his doing? So Paul writes that "he made himself nothing . . . he humbled himself, and in obedience accepted even death — death on a cross" (Phil. 2:7f.). How cruelly, then, he must have felt the ignorant mockery that was so savagely hurled at him as he hung on the cross: "Come down from the cross and save yourself, if you are indeed the Son of God . . . . He saved others, but he cannot save himself. Let him come down now from the cross, and then we will believe in him. Did he trust in God? Let God rescue him, if he wants him — for he said he was God's Son" (Matt. 27:40-43). Such jibes must have pierced his heart more painfully than the nails pierced his flesh.

But, as we have already observed, it was for this very hour that the Son had come into our world. It was, for him, the hour of achievement, in which the purpose of his coming was fulfilled. In view of this, his final word from the cross, "It is accomplished!" (John 19:30), has a very special significance: with his sacrificial death at Calvary the redemption he had come to provide was completed. The hour of Christ's death, no less than the hour of his birth, was appointed by God: not until the time had fully come did he send his Son to be born and to die for us (Gal. 4:4). This consideration explains the remarkable fact that the adversaries of Jesus were unable to lay violent hands on him until the destined hour had arrived, though they made repeated attempts to do so. "They tried to seize him," John recounts, "but no one laid a hand on him because his appointed hour had not yet come." When temple police were sent to arrest him they returned to the chief priests and Pharisees empty-handed. Despite the presence of Jesus, apparently de-fenseless, in their midst, those who wished to harm him found themselves mysteriously restrained from doing so (John 7:30, 32, 44ff.; 8:20, 59; 10:39). Only when his hour had come were they permitted to do with him as they pleased. God, in other words, was in control of all that took place, even of their wickedness and defiance.

This striking perspective is quite clearly that of the apostolic church. Peter, for example, asserted on the day of Pentecost that the killing of Jesus by lawless men was *"according to the deliberate will and plan of God"* (Acts 2:23). Shortly afterwards, the disciples, threatened with severe punishment if they continued to proclaim the Christian gospel, unitedly prayed to God as the Almighty Creator of the whole universe: "Sovereign Lord, maker of heaven and earth and sea and of everything in them" — an invocation which immediately reduces their situation to its proper proportion, for if God is the supreme Creator and Governor of all then the threats of mortal men against his servants are seen to be altogether ludicrous. They recalled the words of Psalm 2 — "Why did the Gentiles rage and the people lay their plots in vain? The kings of the earth took their stand and the rulers made common cause against the Lord and against his Messiah" — and they perceived how precisely these words applied to the manner in which Jesus, God's holy Servant and Messiah, was treated: "They did indeed make common cause in this very city against thy holy servant Jesus whom thou didst anoint as Messiah. Herod and Pon-tius Pilate conspired with the Gentiles and peoples of Israel to do . . . ." To do what? Certainly, they conspired to do what was thoroughly evil and unjust; but the apostolic gaze penetrated beyond the merely human scene and discerned the hand of God at work sovereignly overruling in all that took place. And so their prayer continued: ". . . *to do all the things which, under thy hand and by thy decree, were fore-ordained*" (Acts 4:24-28). This is exactly the opposite of what the adversaries of Christ intended. Thus God's control over all things for the setting forward of his purposes, and the futility of all opposition to the divine will were plainly demonstrated. "Surely," says Paul, "the Potter can do what he likes with the clay" (Rom. 9:21).

THE RECONCILIATION OF ALL THINGS

The redemption provided by God in Christ Jesus is concentrated on man as the crown of the created order, but the effect of this redemption extends beyond man and through man to the whole world over which man was originally placed to exercise dominion in accordance with the Creator's will and to his glory. As we noticed in the preceding chapter, man in falling away from God through disobedience and ingratitude has dragged down the rest of creation with him, with the result that the entire created order is depicted as longing to participate in the renewal promised by Christ's redemption (Rom. 8:19ff.). Conversely, therefore, the restoration of man leads inevitably to the restoration of all things. When at last, thanks to the redeeming grace of God, mankind faithfully discharges the mandate to govern the rest of creation in accordance with the divine will, it follows that peace and harmony will return to the whole. Thus Peter speaks of "the time of universal restoration" (Acts 3:21);

and Paul refers to the same truth when he says that in Christ God was reconciling *the world* to himself (II Cor. 5:19). God's "hidden purpose . . . determined beforehand in Christ" was that, at precisely the right moment, "the universe, all in heaven and on earth, should be brought into a unity in Christ" (Eph. 1:9f.). Or again, as Paul puts it in another place, "through his Son God chose to reconcile the whole universe to himself, making peace through the shedding of his blood upon the cross — to reconcile all things, whether on earth or in heaven, through him alone" (Col. 1:20).

The renewal of the divine image in man promises the renewal of the whole of creation. Hence it is not surprising to find that Paul is fond of using the language of creation when speaking of regeneration in Christ. It is as though the atoning work of Christ brings about a fresh creation. "If any man be in Christ," he writes, "he is a new creation: old things have passed away; behold, they have become new" (II Cor. 5:17). "The same God who said [at creation], 'Out of darkness let light shine,' has caused his light to shine within us, to give the light of revelation — the revelation of the glory of God in the face of Jesus Christ" (II Cor. 4:6). The members of the Ephesian church are exhorted to "put on the new nature, created after the likeness of God in true righteousness and holiness" — which in other words is the renewal of the image in which man was first created (Eph. 4:24); indeed, they have already been reminded that they are "God's handiwork, created in Christ Jesus to devote ourselves to the good deeds for which God has designed us" (Eph. 2:10). The Christian believer, Paul affirms, has "put on the new nature, which is being constantly renewed in the image of its Creator" (Col. 3:10), thus, by the grace of God, fulfilling his destiny, namely, to be "conformed to the image of his Son" (Rom. 8:29).[4] Beholding the glory of the Lord, he is "transformed into the same image from glory to glory" (II Cor. 3:18). Thanks to the sanctifying work of the Holy Spirit, the beauty of the authentic Image of his creation is progressively restored ("from glory to glory"), until at last the new-man-in-Christ attains the perfection of manhood, that is, until he arrives at "the full stature of Christ" (Eph. 4:13). This creative, or re-creative, transformation will achieve completion when the Redeemer returns in glory at the end of the age: "We know," says John, "that when he appears we shall be like him, because we shall see him as he is." The moment of this beatific encounter is therefore the moment of the total conformity of our humanity to the likeness of him who is the true Image and the true destiny of our creation. Meanwhile, "everyone who has this hope in Christ purifies himself, even as he is pure" (I John 3:2f.).

As Creator, as Sustainer, and as Redeemer, God's supremacy over all his works is complete. The sovereignty of his control is absolute — and necessarily so. Otherwise we cease to speak about God. His purposes cannot fail. His will is not subject to chance or the unknown. He determines the end as well as the beginning. The choosing of his people takes place in Christ before the world's foundation (Eph. 1:4). The Christian, no matter how severe his trials and afflictions may be, is fully assured that God causes all things to work together for the good of those whom he has called, for his calling is also his enabling. And this calling is preceded by God's foreknowledge and foreordination, just as it is accompanied by justification and leads on to glorification. To be called by God according to his purpose is to be lifted into

---

4. In the expression "the image of his Son" the meaning is "the image that is his Son," if we take the genitive as a genitive of apposition.

CHAPTER FOUR
The Judgment of Man

God, we have been saying, is sovereign not only as the Creator, who has brought all things into existence and providentially sustains them in accordance with his creative will and purpose, but also as the Redeemer, who through the incarnation and death of the eternal Son has taken decisive action against the evil by which our world has been invaded. The Son's conquest of death was attested by his resurrection from the grave, and his glorious exaltation was at the same time the glorious exaltation of our humanity which he had taken to himself. In him who is the true Image after which man was created the fulness of our humanity is restored and our destiny assured; and by virtue of the inward working of the Holy Spirit, who applies the benefits of his saving work to the believing heart, the gospel of Jesus Christ proves powerful to transform human lives and human society, bringing light in place of darkness, purpose in place of lostness, joy in place of sorrow, fellowship in place of alienation, and hope in place of despair. The remedy, in short, for all the world's ills is ready at hand thanks to God's redemptive intervention through Christ Jesus.

This is all very fine as far as it goes, someone may respond, but the hard fact still remains that the world is in the deplorable state described in the earlier part of this book. Even though it is true that, as Paul says, when the Son's reconciling mission was completed "God raised him to the heights and bestowed on him the name above all names, that at the name of Jesus every knee should bow — in heaven, on earth, and in the depths — and every tongue confess, 'Jesus Christ is Lord,' to the glory of God the Father" (Phil. 2:9-11), it is all too evident that the name of Jesus is not universally honored and that peace and harmony among men are far from being established. The Christian gospel may be the solution to the world's problems, but it can hardly be said to have brought about the transformation that is needed. Why is it that things continue as they are even after the completion of God's atoning work in Christ?

THE FINAL AGE

In proposing an answer to this question there is more than one factor that must be taken into consideration. In the first place, though this divine intervention through Christ is regarded in the biblical perspective as absolutely unique and decisive, it does not mark the end of human history but rather its mid-point. All that precedes it leads up to it, and all that follows derives special significance from it. It is indeed the pivot or hinge of human history. So crucial is this event that it introduces "the last days" (Joel 2:28; Acts 2:17) which constitute "the final age" (Heb. 1:2; I Peter 1:20; I John 2:18). The coming of the Son into the world is the very "climax of history" (Heb. 9:26) which casts its light both backwards and forwards and gives meaning and relevance to the whole.

"It is already the time of the end, and yet is not *the* end,"

Oscar Cullmann writes. "This tension finds expression in the entire theology of Primitive Christianity. The present period of the Church is the time between the decisive battle, which has already occurred, and the 'Victory Day.' "[1] The critical defeat of the enemy took place at Calvary, but the warfare continues against an enemy who is desperate and dangerous. The end is "not yet" but, no matter how long it may be delayed, it is always "near at hand" (Mark 13:7; James 5:3; I Peter 4:7). The Christian, who is invited to share in the joy of his Lord's victory banquet (Luke 14:15ff.; Rev. 19:9), is exhorted first to endure hardship "like a good soldier of Jesus Christ" (II Tim. 2:3). The victory achieved at Christ's first coming will have its culmination at his second coming, which will mark the conclusion of these "last days" and the dawn of the "eternal day" of God's unclouded glory (Rom. 13:12; Rev. 21:23ff.). The triumphant appearance of the Son at the end of this age brings not only the fulness of his people's salvation but also the final judgment and elimination of the enemy and his forces (Rev. 20:11ff.). This present final age therefore is bounded by the two comings of Christ, and this explains why it is a period characterized by the tension of "already" and "not yet." Believers are "already," "here and now" enriched by Christ in all things; they are even now the children of God, but the completion of their salvation is "not yet" and is still to be revealed (I Cor. 1:5; I John 3:2); the truth they see "now" they see imperfectly, but "then" they will see face to face; "now" their knowledge is partial, but "then" they will know fully even as they are known by God (I Cor. 13:12f.). Satan has "already" been judged, together with his ungodly followers,

---

1. Oscar Cullmann, *Christ and Time*, pp. 145f.

but the execution of the sentence of final destruction has "not yet" been carried out (John 16:11; 12:31; 3:18f.; Col. 2:15; II Thess. 1:6ff.; II Peter 2:3). For them, too, these are "the last days"; for them these last days will end, however, not in glory but in perdition.

Second, the full effect of God's redemptive intervention through Christ is still a reality of the future because the good news of this divine provision for our restoration must first be proclaimed to all people throughout the length and breadth of the world. When Jesus told his disciples, "The end is not yet," he also said: "This gospel of the Kingdom will be proclaimed throughout the earth as a testimony to all nations; and then the end will come" (Matt. 24:7, 14; Mark 13:10). Accordingly, the ascending Savior's final commission to his followers is one of world-wide evangelization: "You will receive power when the Holy Spirit comes upon you; and you will bear witness for me in Jerusalem, and all over Judea and Samaria, and away to the ends of the earth" (Acts 1:8); and with this commission he gives them the promise: "Be assured, I am with you always, to the end of the age" (Matt. 28:19f.). In other words, this period between the two comings of Christ is the era of evangelism in which the church has been entrusted with the specific task of preaching the gospel everywhere and to all, because it is the message of God's saving power to everyone who receives it with faith (Rom. 1:16). Thus the era of evangelism is also the era of opportunity for the world to hear and respond to the good news of God's grace in Jesus Christ: these "last days" are the age of grace.

To conclude from the persistence of evil and injustice in the world that God is incompetent to set things right and that his promises are empty of meaning and power is, then, a total, and indeed a fatal, misreading of the situation.

Peter speaks of the arrogance of scoffers who, because they see no evidence of the promised restoration of all things, say: "Where is now the promise of his coming? Our fathers have been laid to rest, but still everything continues exactly as it has always been since the world began." And the apostle replies to this criticism with the following admonition:

> Here is one point, my friends, which you must not lose sight of: with the Lord one day is like a thousand years and a thousand years like one day. It is not that the Lord is slow in fulfilling his promise, as some suppose, but that he is very patient with you, because it is not his will for any to be lost, but for all to come to repentance. (II Peter 3:3-9)

The delay of final judgment is not a sign of weakness on God's part but an evidence, rather, of his gracious forbearance.

EVANGELISM AND RESPONSIBILITY

But the opportunity of hearing the gospel which this age of evangelism affords is accompanied by the responsibility of receiving or rejecting the new life that is offered in Christ. To reject it is to "condemn oneself as unworthy of eternal life" (Acts 13:46); to receive it is to find reconciliation and "peace through the shedding of Christ's blood upon the cross" (Col. 1:20). The responsibility therefore is a solemn one, for eternal issues are involved. The author of the Epistle to the Hebrews warns his readers of the danger of following the "evil example of unbelief" of the Israelites in the wilderness who hardened their hearts against the grace and the goodness of God, with the result that that whole generation perished there in the wilderness instead of entering into the rest awaiting God's people in the promised land. He cites the admonition of the Psalmist: "Today if you hear his voice, do not grow stubborn as in those days of rebellion" (Ps. 95:7f.), urging that it is still "Today," that is, the "day" of God's patience and thus the "day" of opportunity for us to turn from our faithless ingratitude and from the dominion of Satan in response to the grace of God freely available to us in Christ Jesus (Heb. 3:7ff.; Acts 26:18). The alternative to salvation and life is damnation and death. Of false teachers Peter bluntly says that "perdition waits for them with un-sleeping eyes." He points out that God did not spare the angels who sinned, nor the old world of godless men which, with the exception of Noah, the "preacher of righteous-ness," and his family, was overwhelmed by the flood, nor did God spare the cities of Sodom and Gomorrah which, while Lot, "that righteous man," was rescued, were burned to ashes; and Peter draws attention to the plain conclusion that "the Lord is well able to rescue the godly out of trials, and to reserve the wicked under punishment until the day of judgment" (II Peter 2:3-9).

Third, as we seek to understand the confused state of the world in the light of the biblical perspective it is important to recognize that redemption implies judgment. The pro-longation of this final age does not mean that the ungodly are somehow managing to escape God's ultimate judgment. Salvation has no meaning if there is nothing from which we need to be saved, and God's redeeming work in Christ was necessary precisely because mankind, fallen and sinful, lay under the cloud of divine judgment. There is nothing in-congruous about associating the wrath of God with the cross of Christ, though it is true that the cross of Christ is the supreme manifestation of the love of God. Indeed the love of God at Calvary can be properly appreciated only in the closest connection with the irreducible holiness of God. The firmness of divine law and the warmth of divine love are not and cannot be two irreconcilable opposites — the one harsh and rigid, the other flexible and benevolent. Notions of this kind conceive an impossible dualism within the divine nature, not dissimilar in effect from the dualism of ancient paganism, which postulated two "gods," one evil and the other good. But as there can be but one God, one infinite and absolute Being, so it is one and the same God who at the same time and at all times is both holy and loving. The schizophrenia of our fallen humanity has no place in the mind of God.

It is man's guilty dread of divine judgment that makes him wish vainly to eliminate the attribute of holy righteousness from the nature of God. Aware of his own unrighteousness and its deserts, the ungodly man fashions for himself a picture of God as solely a loving Father. He would like above all to be rid of the truth that God is a just Judge. But justice belongs to the very fabric of creation. It interpenetrates every aspect of man's existence. In a society where crime and violence flourish unchecked human dignity suffers a monstrous affront. The judicial system, which in one form or another is found in every country of the world, condemns and punishes the guilty, and necessarily so if men are to live together with any degree of sanity. This common recognition of the need for the exercise of justice is itself a reflection of the justice of God, who is the source not only of all life and knowledge but also of all authority. Paul even describes those who administer civil authority, commending welldoing and punishing wrongdoing, as ministers of God (Rom. 13:6). Moreover, the distinction between right and wrong operates at every level of the social structure. A good government is one that is just and impartial; business and trade are expected to be honorably conducted; schools should function in accordance with approved standards of learning and behavior; the happy family is one in which there is adequate discipline and mutual respect; and, as we have mentioned earlier, it is accepted by all that even sporting contests and the simplest games must be played with respect for the rules, and with suitable penalties for infractions. This pervasive awareness of right and wrong, fair and foul, shows that we instinctively recognize judgment as a necessary part of everyday life; and it is pervasive because we belong to a moral universe.

LAW AND LOVE NOT INCOMPATIBLE

The injustices that we deplore in the world cry out for judgment. This is generally agreed. But this agreement makes no sense if there is no absolute standard of justice and no supreme judge. It is in effect an acknowledgment both of the necessity and of the inevitability of ultimate judgment. Now if we, finite and fallen though we are and too frequently unjust in our dealings with others, have this sense of what is right and just, then there is an undeniable force in Abraham's rhetorical question: "Shall not the Judge of all the earth do what is just?" (Gen. 18:25). By his very constitution in the divine image man knows very well that his Creator is a God of justice (Isa. 30:18), who "will judge the world with righteousness" (Ps. 96:13). This is a truth of the greatest importance, but it is no less important that we should clearly understand that the affirmation of God's absolute justice in no sense diminishes the reality of the full perfection of his love.

So far from law and love being incompatible with each other, they belong inseparably together. The keeping of the law is synonymous with the life of love. Thus the summary of the Ten Commandments is this: "Love the Lord your God with all your heart, with all your soul, with all your strength, and with all your mind; and your neighbour as yourself" (Luke 10:26f.); and Paul says (referring in particular to the second table of the law): "He who loves his neighbour has satisfied every claim of the law . . . Love cannot wrong a neighbour; therefore the whole law is summed up in love" (Rom. 13:8-10; cf. I Cor. 13). The love of God in redeeming mankind does not require the setting aside of the justice of God. If it did, it would have the extraordinary and incredible consequence that God would be divided against himself as he is faced with the dilemma of having to be unjust to be loving or having to be unloving to be just.

We should not be surprised that the cross, when divorced from the righteous judgment of God against sin, becomes an immoral spectacle. The so-called "subjective" theory of the atonement which denies the necessity of the cross and rejects the conception of Christ's death as a satisfaction for sin, maintaining that it is solely a demonstration of God's love intended to melt our hard hearts and move us to repentance, betrays an inadequate view both of the seriousness of sin and its effects and also of the holiness of God. It leaves the love of God in the disconnectedness of a vacuum. In fact, in separating the cross of Calvary from the sphere of justice it also separates it from the sphere of love, transforming it, rather, into a cruel and grotesque exhibition of the senseless, because unnecessary, suffering of the innocent, which should repel rather than attract the one who contemplates it. The cause of love is not served by injustice. "If we spoke less about God's love and more about his holiness, more about his judgment," P. T. Forsyth has well said, "we should say much more when we did speak of his love"; indeed, "the holiness of God is a deeper revelation in the cross than his love, for it is what gives his love divine value" — so much so, that his love "is meaningless without judgment."[2] Similarly, Martyn Lloyd-Jones has written:

> It is only in the light of God's hatred and abhorrence of sin that we can really see his love and appreciate the wonder and glory of the gospel . . . . The love of God is a holy love. It expresses itself not by condoning sin or compromising with it; it deals with it, and yet does so in such a way that the sinner is not destroyed with his sin, but is delivered from it and its consequences.[3]

And Paul expressly states that by Christ's sacrificial death "God meant to demonstrate his justice, . . . showing that he is himself just and also justifies any man who puts his faith in Jesus" (Rom. 3:25f.).

Conversely, of course, if the cross is divorced from the overflowing love of God for the sinner it becomes a cold and unloving spectacle. An "objective" view of the atonement which supposes that at Calvary the angry Father is striking down his helpless Son betrays a terrible misunderstanding of what was really taking place there, and can only have the effect of saddling God, again, with a split personality. God is the One God: as we have already seen, there can be no disharmony in his will or in his work. What the Father wills the Son wills; what the Son does the Father does. The Father's giving up of the Son for us is the highest summit of all love. The truth is this, that "God loved so much that he gave his only Son" (John 3:16). The fact that "Christ died for us while we were yet sinners" is "God's own proof of his love towards us" (Rom. 5:8). It was actually God who was reconciling the world to himself in Christ (II Cor. 5:19).

---

2. P. T. Forsyth, *The Cruciality of the Cross,* pp. 39, 98.

3. D. Martyn Lloyd-Jones, *The Plight of Man and the Power of God,* pp. 74f.

What we see at the cross is the perfect union of divine love and divine justice.

THE CENTRALITY OF THE CROSS

The death of Christ, moreover, was not the death of a faithful martyr powerless to avert the fury of malicious men, nor was it the death of a tragic hero overtaken by an inexorable fate beyond his control, such as we find in the classical drama of Greece. It was the death of *God incarnate:* a great mystery, indeed, but in this truth lies the reality and the power of the cross to save our sinful humanity; for God incarnate is God in action, God in control, even as he is nailed to the cross to die there, God sovereignly by death breaking the dominion of Satan and rescuing mankind from the clutch of death (Heb. 2:14f.). The cross is the place where the judgment of God against our sin was poured out: in this the holy righteousness of God is displayed. But the amazing thing is that there that divine judgment was poured out not on us but on him who is God incarnate — and this means that at Calvary God in Christ not only exercised but also himself endured his own judgment in our stead. To quote P. T. Forsyth again: God "must either inflict punishment or assume it. And he chose the latter course, as honouring the law while saving the guilty. He took his own judgment."[4] We can never doubt the pure and boundless nature of God's love, nor the adamantine holiness of his justice, once we understand that on the cross he himself, in the person of the incarnate Son, absorbed the punishment due to our sin.

---

4. P. T. Forsyth, *The Cruciality of the Cross,* p. 98.

Precisely and only because it is the *locus* of judgment the cross is the *locus* of salvation. It is the throne of divine grace because it is the seat of divine judgment. The Son did not come to judge the world, but to save the world (John 12:47); but he saved the world by himself being judged in our stead and for our sins (I John 2:2); and on the cross he not only removed our judgment by enduring it but he also made available to us the perfection of his righteousness, so that in him we might stand justified before God (Rom. 3:26; 5:1ff.).

In the light of this truth, the absolute centrality of the cross of Christ is obvious. Because the cross is the place and the "moment" of God's sovereign intervention for the saving of the world it is the central focal point of all human history. It is the witness to God's power both to judge and to redeem. It confirms that God the holy Judge is also God the loving Redeemer. Christ crucified is the center and heart of the good news which is proclaimed throughout the world (Rom. 1:16f.; I Cor. 1:23; 2:2; Gal. 6:14). And it is by their response, either of faith or of disobedience, to what God has done at Calvary that men are either justified or condemned before their Creator (John 3:16-19, 36). This means that the cross, though properly God's instrument of salvation, becomes God's instrument of judgment in the case of those who reject the salvation it offers. P. T. Forsyth, who had so profound an appreciation of the holiness of God's grace, laid great stress on this truth:

> The absolute ultimate judgment of the world took place in Christ's death. There God spoke his last word — his last endless word. The last moral reality is there, the last standard, the last judgment. The last judgment is behind us. The true judgment-seat of Christ, where we must all appear, is the cross . . . . It was only by judgment that salvation could come; it was our judgment fallen on Christ that was our salvation; and it is this salvation that is our worst judgment

. . . . Our worst condemnation is not that we have sinned, but that we have refused to be saved from our sin.[5]

There is nothing surprising about this conception of the cross as the event with reference to which mankind will be either saved or judged. Salvation flows from the cross because there the incarnate Son bore the divine judgment against the sins of the whole world (I John 2:2). The proclamation of this good news throughout the world is the task of evangelism in this final age between the two comings of Christ. Condemnation flows from this same cross against all who reject the gospel and refuse to accept what God has graciously done for them in Christ. By turning away from the judgment that Christ bore for them they retain that judgment for themselves: they invite the wrath of God to rest upon them (John 3:36). Thus the cross is always the source both of justification and of condemnation. Because it is the work of God it is never ineffective. The gospel is double-edged; or, as Paul says, using the imagery of the Roman triumphal procession, Christ's messengers "everywhere spread abroad the fragrance" of the gospel, "both for those who are on the way to salvation, and for those who are on the way to perdition: to the latter it is a deadly fume that kills, to the former a vital fragrance that brings life" (II Cor. 2:15f.).

This double action belongs to all that God says and does on behalf of man. There is no area of neutrality or inaction. The cross of Christ is God's action for our salvation, but it becomes a means of perdition for those who deny its power. The flood was God's action of judgment on the godless generation of Noah's day, but it was at the same time the means of salvation for Noah and the company in the ark

---

5. P. T. Forsyth, *Missions in State and Church,* pp. 61f., 73f.

with him who "were brought to safety through the water" (I Peter 3:20). The sacrament of the eucharist was instituted by Christ as a means of grace for his followers, but those who eat the bread and drink the cup of the Lord unworthily eat and drink judgment on themselves (I Cor. 11:27-29). So also God's ultimate intervention, when the victorious Redeemer returns at the end of this age, will bring the execution of final judgment on all who persist in unbelief and, simultaneously, the consummating glory of salvation for all who welcome their Lord's appearing (II Tim. 4:8). This, the Day of the Lord, will be for all either a day of joy or a day of doom. *The same day* that Noah entered the security of the ark "the flood came and made an end of them all"; and *the same day* that Lot was rescued from Sodom "it rained fire and sulphur from the sky and made an end of them all": so, Christ taught, "it will be like that on the day when the Son of Man is revealed" (Luke 17:26-30).

GOD'S FINAL INTERVENTION

This day of the Son's glorious manifestation will mark the end of the age and will also be God's final intervention in the course of human history. It will be the harvest day when God's people are gathered in, like wheat, to enjoy endless bliss in his presence, and when the ungodly, like useless weeds, are cast out and destroyed. Meanwhile the eternal destinies of all are being determined in accordance with their response of faith or disobedience to God's central redemptive intervention in Christ. Wheat and darnel "both grow together till harvest," when at last the ultimate separation will unerringly be made (Matt. 13:24-30, 36-43). A dragnet catches fish of every kind and a separation has to be made between the good and the worthless: "That is how it will be at the end of time. The angels will go forth, and they will separate the wicked from the good, and throw them into the blazing furnace, the place of wailing and grinding of teeth" (Matt. 13:47-50). Moreover, for the good seed of the gospel to spring up and produce a harvest it is necessary for it to fall into good soil. Christ's parable of the sower is confirmed by the fortunes of evangelism: some people have no place at all in their hearts for the message of redemption; others accept it with signs of gladness but without allowing it to take root in their lives, "then, when there is trouble or persecution on account of the word, they fall away at once"; in others the word seems to find a lodgment, but after a while, like thistles, "worldly cares and the false glamour of wealth and all kinds of evil desire come in and choke the word, and it proves barren"; but there are others who receive the good seed into the good soil of believing and grateful hearts, and who bring forth a harvest to the glory of God (Mark 4:3-20; John 15:8).

In the light of these considerations, we see why it is that evil and corruption are still present in the world, that godless men and antichristian movements continue to vaunt themselves, and that hypocrites are found in the membership of the church. The gospel is being given time to operate; the period of God's grace is being prolonged; lives are being transformed by the dynamic of that grace; others are hardening themselves in enmity to the cross; until at last the salvation and the judgment that are now active will be universally declared at the appearing of him who, according as he is each person's Redeemer or Judge now, will then make the final and irrevocable separation. It is only to be expected that as this day of reckoning approaches the forces of evil should seek to assert themselves with growing fury and desperation. As their time is short so their defiance mounts. Their fate is sealed, the judgment is sure, and at God's next decisive intervention the sentence of their destruction will be executed.

If the first coming of Christ, and in particular the cross which was the purpose of that coming, is (because of its cosmic significance) the turning point or fulcrum of all history and God's answer to all that is wrong in human society, it is essential that there should be a terminus or omega point towards which history is moving and at which the destiny of the whole created order will be achieved. For things to continue as they are, marred by discord and injustice and frustrated by sickness and death, generation after generation without end would be ultimately meaningless. It would leave the cross a dark symbol without power or glory. It would prove the weakness or the unrighteousness of God. It would destroy the conviction of the moral and rational structure of the universe. Human existence would be a speck of foam in the vortex of despair. But such a perspective is impossible for man — for every man, even for those who call themselves nihilists. It is impossible because, as we have seen, man is God's creature, made in the divine image, so that he knows, by his very constitution, that God exists and is sovereign over the whole of his creation, including human society. And it is impossible, also, because God has decisively intervened for the redemption of his fallen creation by the sending of his Son into the world to die for sins, Man for man, to rise from the grave as the triumphant Lord of Life, and to be exalted as the King of Glory to whom every knee shall bow.

To speak like this is not to indulge in theological

speculation. What God has done in Christ is a matter of history — not just God's history: it was done *for man*, and it took place within human history. We know the time and the place. We have the testimony of eyewitnesses. But above all we have the witness of the Holy Spirit which, thanks to the outpouring at Pentecost, is a universal witness and an inward witness which accompanies the proclamation of the gospel throughout the whole world, a witness, indeed, which convinces men of the truth of the gospel and convicts those who persist in unbelief of their guilt and of the divine judgment that awaits them (John 16:8-11). God's action in Christ, moreover, is not merely a matter of past history, for, as we have explained above, its cosmic significance and power are such as to determine the destiny of all men, whether unto life or unto perdition. In this age of evangelism and opportunity it is the special work of the Holy Spirit to make God's action in Christ fully real and existential in the experience of men. There is, consequently, the contemporary evidence, the present history, of human lives totally and gloriously transformed by the power of God through the reception, by faith, of the new life that is freely offered in Christ Jesus. The Christian message is a *dynamic* message. The dynamism of the gospel is the dynamism of the Holy Spirit, and this dynamism, once experienced, becomes also the essential dynamism of the Christian's evangelistic witness to the world. That is why Paul assures his Thessalonian readers: "When we brought you the gospel, we brought it not in mere words but in the power of the Holy Spirit and with strong conviction" (I Thess. 1:5). "The word I spoke, the gospel I proclaimed, did not sway you with subtle arguments," he writes to his converts in Corinth; "it carried conviction by spiritual power, so that your faith might be built not upon human wisdom but upon the power of God" (I Cor. 2:4f.).

THE CONSUMMATION OF HUMAN HISTORY

God has decreed an end as well as a beginning, a fulfilment as well as a development. History has meaning precisely because it is moving on towards a conclusion sovereignly predetermined by God. "God now commands mankind, all men everywhere, to repent," the apostle Paul told his audience of philosophers in Athens, "because he has fixed the day on which he will have the world judged, by a man of his choosing; of this he has given assurance to all by raising him from the dead" (Acts 17:30f.). The consummation of human history will coincide with the glorious manifestation of Christ at the end of this age: the dreadful hour of judgment for those who have spurned the gospel, but the hour of inexpressible joy for those who greet him as Savior and Lord. "Christ has appeared once and for all at the climax of history to abolish sin by the sacrifice of himself," says the author of the Epistle to the Hebrews. "And as it is the lot of men to die once, and after death comes judgment, so Christ was offered once to bear the burden of men's sins, and will appear a second time, sin done away, to bring salvation to those who are watching for him" (Heb. 9:26-28). In other words, when Christ comes the second time he is not coming to die the second time. The death he died at Calvary is all-sufficient and therefore once-for-all, and when he returns the judgment he bore for others at his first coming will be the judgment he wields against all who have rejected him as their sin-bearer. For such, "no sacrifice for sins remains: only a terrifying expectation of judgment" (Heb. 10:26f.). For others, the moment of their Lord's appearing means the realization of the fulness of their salvation (cf. Luke 21:28; Rom. 13:11).

The second advent of the Son will be very different from the first, for it will not be a coming marked by humiliation and suffering, but a coming in power and majesty. He is still, indeed, the incarnate Son, but now exalted and glorified, and our humanity is exalted and glorified in him and with him. The day of his coming will be his wedding day, when his bride the church will be united to him and will share his glory for evermore, for it will mean the union of our humanity with the holy humanity that is his and its transfiguration by the radiance of his presence. Then this jubilant cry will rise from the multitude of his redeemed:

> Alleluia! The Lord our God, sovereign over all, has entered on his reign! Exult and shout for joy and do him homage, for the wedding-day of the Lamb has come! His bride has made herself ready, and for her dress she has been given fine linen, clean and shining. (Rev. 19:6-8)

But the day of his coming will also be the day of final reckoning, when he whose name is the Word of God and Faithful and True rides forth as King of kings and Lord of lords to smite his enemies with an iron rod and to "tread the winepress of the wrath and retribution of God the sovereign Lord" (Rev. 19:11-16).

THE DESTINY OF CREATION

Thus the "new heaven and new earth" are ushered in. The renewal of the whole of creation involves not only the exclusion and destruction of all who would defile it by their ungodliness, but also the raising of man (and with and under him the created order) to that higher dimension of blessedness which was always intended as his destiny. The creation will be fully attuned to the perfection of God himself and purified by his holy presence. It will be populated by the "vast multitude which no man can number, from every nation, of all tribes, peoples, and languages," of those who "have washed their robes and made them white in the blood of the Lamb" and who joyfully and ceaselessly praise and serve God, free from all sorrow, suffering, and death (Rev. 7:9-17). For then the proclamation will be heard:

> Now at last God has his dwelling among men! He will dwell among them and they shall be his people, and God himself will be with them. He will wipe every tear from their eyes; there shall be an end to death, and to mourning and crying and pain; for the old order has passed away! (Rev. 21:3f.)

Mankind, redeemed and glorified, drinks fully of the river of the water of life and eats freely of the tree of life, which were lost through sin and disobedience but now are regained through union with him who is Life itself (Rev. 22:1ff.; John 14:6).

All that was forfeited through man's rebellion against God is now restored — and more, for the purpose for which all was created now achieves its fulfilment. Now at last completely conformed to that Image after which he was made, man attains the full potential of his humanity as, in harmony with the divine will, he exercises dominion over a world that is mature and free from blemish. In accordance with the assurance that "every accursed thing shall disappear" (Rev. 22:3), all illness and disease, all corruption and injustice, all violence and bloodshed, all grief and death itself, everything in short by which human life and society is at present blighted is dispelled and destroyed, never to be seen again. The days of hard toil and pilgrimage now behind them, and their wilderness journey completed, the people of God enter into the eternal enjoyment of the rest of the Creator's seventh day, a day of undimmed glory and threatened by no darkness, for it is a day without evening in which redeemed mankind walks always in the pure light of him who himself is eternal Light (I John 1:7; Rev. 21:23f.).

The sovereign power and goodness of God will thus be vindicated and made manifest to all in the perfect order and beatific harmony of the renewed creation. The reign of love and justice will be everlastingly established and all will be blessed with eternal peace by the Lord of peace (cf. II Thess. 3:16). The great company of the redeemed who are the citizens of the new world will be filled with inexpressible joy and satisfaction as, delighting in the divine will, they give themselves ceaselessly to the service of God, and as they are constantly enraptured by the marvelous beauty of all his works. The far vision of the Psalmist who desired that everything that has breath should praise the Lord (Ps. 150:6) now becomes reality as all creatures unite in adoration: "Praise and honour, glory and might, to him who sits on the throne and to the Lamb for ever and ever!" (Rev. 5:13). For all will now be gloriously unified and integrated in Christ and the worship and wonder of all will be for ever fresh. The anticipation of such bliss caused Richard Baxter to exclaim:

> Have the gales of grace blown me into such a harbour: is it hither that Christ hath enticed my soul? O blessed way, and thrice blessed end! . . . O vile nature, that resisted so much and so long such a blessing: unworthy soul! Is this the place thou camest so unwillingly towards: was duty wearisome; was the world too good to lose? Didst thou stick at leaving all, denying all, and suffering anything for this: wast thou loath to die to come to this? . . . Now art thou sufficiently convinced that the ways thou calledst hard, and the cup thou calledst bitter, were necessary; that thy Lord hath sweeter ends and meant thee better than thou wouldest believe; and that thy Redeemer was saving thee as well when he crossed thy desires as when he granted them, and as well when he broke thy heart as when he bound it up. O, no thanks to thee, unworthy self, but shame, for this received crown; but to Jehovah and the Lamb be glory for ever![6]

---

6. Richard Baxter, *The Saint's Everlasting Rest,* i.4.

THE FULFILMENT OF ALL GOD'S PURPOSES

And so all the purposes of God are brought to fruition.
Because the work of creation, being the work *of God,* could
not fail and come to nothing, the end was in the beginning —
indeed, the end was assured by the beginning. Moreover, the
work of re-creation, which is the means of bringing the
beginning to the end, could not fail or come to nothing
because it was the work *of God.* In the consummation of all
things, accordingly, the beginning is in the end. That blessed
life from which man was expelled because of his sin is now
his again thanks to God's grace in Christ Jesus. The gates are
no longer barred, but wide open once more for that in-
numerable company that knows the cleansing power of the
Savior's atoning blood: "Happy are those who wash their
robes clean! They will have the right to the tree of life and
will enter by the gates of the city" (Rev. 22:14; cf. Gen.
3:23f.). Not only the constitution of all things but also their
reconstitution is God's work in and through the eternal Son,
the Living One who as the incarnate Son died on the cross
and now is alive for evermore (Rev. 1:18). The Son is "the
first principle of all God's creation" (Rev. 3:14), and in him
"the universe, all in heaven and earth," has its destined consummation (Eph. 1:10). But he who is "the Alpha and the
Omega, the first and the last, the beginning and the end"
(Rev. 22:13) is also, as Mediator (I Tim. 2:5f.), the center,
the one through whom the beginning is linked to and
achieves the end. It is through Christ, Paul declares, that
"God chose to reconcile the whole universe to himself,

making peace through the shedding of his blood upon the cross — to reconcile all things, whether on earth or in heaven, through him alone" (Col. 1:20). In Christ, therefore, the whole of creation, and not least our humanity, which under the Creator is the heart and mind of the cosmos, attains its resplendent destiny, and all the purposes and promises of God are brought to majestic fulfilment. No wonder John in his vision heard the myriad hosts of creation in unison praising their glorified Redeemer: "Worthy is the Lamb, the Lamb that was slain, to receive all power and wealth, wisdom and might, honour and glory and praise!" (Rev. 5:12); and well may we join with the poet in his desire:

> That we on Earth with undiscording voice
> May rightly answer that melodious noise:
> As once we did, till disproportion'd sin
> Jarr'd against nature's chime, and with harsh din
> Broke the fair music that all creatures made
> To their great Lord, whose love their motion sway'd
> In perfect Diapason, whilst they stood
> In first obedience, and their state of good.
> O may we soon again renew that Song,
> And keep in tune with Heav'n, till God ere long
> To his celestial consort us unite,
> To live with him, and sing in endless morn of light.[7]

---

7. John Milton, "At a Solemn Musick."